C000262580

SAMS
Teach Yourself
Today

e-Real Estate

e-Real Estate

Jack Segner

A Division of Macmillan USA
201 West 103rd Street, Indianapolis, Indiana 46290

Sams Teach Yourself e-Real Estate Today

Copyright ©2000 by Sams Publishing

International Standard Book Number: 0-672-31815-6

Library of Congress Catalog Card Number: 99-067007

Printed in the United States of America

First Printing: December 1999

02   01   00   4   3   2

Trademarks

All terms mentioned in this book that are known to be trademarks or service marks have been appropriately capitalized. Sams Publishing cannot attest to the accuracy of this information. Use of a term in this book should not be regarded as affecting the validity of any trademark or service mark.

Warning and Disclaimer

Every effort has been made to make this book as complete and as accurate as possible, but no warranty or fitness is implied. The information provided is on an "as is" basis. The author and the publisher shall have neither liability nor responsibility to any person or entity with respect to any loss or damages arising from the information contained in this book.

Acquisitions Editor
Jeff Schultz

Development Editor
Alice Martina Smith

Managing Editor
Charlotte Clapp

Project Editor
Christina Smith

Copy Editor
Gene Redding

Indexer
Heather McNeill

Proofreader
Tony Reitz

Team Coordinator
Amy Patton

Interior Designer
Gary Adair

Cover Designer
Jay Corpus

Copy Writer
Eric Borgert

Layout Technicians
Stacey DeRome
Ayanna Lacey
Heather Hiatt Miller

Dedication

To my mother, Barbara Thrower Segner (1920–1999), whose honesty, integrity, and dedication as a real estate professional for over 20 years were exceeded only by her love and devotion as a mother and wife. May you rest in peace and in the knowledge that your goodness lives on and thrives in your grandchildren.

Table of Contents

Part V: Appendixes

Foreword

The Internet has a profound way of changing an industry, and real estate is no exception. With a plethora of real estate–related Web sites (mainly realtors touting how great they are), it's a vastly unorganized web of confusion. The main obstacle has been processing through the mediocre sites to find the relevant information that you need. *Sams Teach Yourself e-Real Estate Today* does exactly that. The book takes you by the hand and wonderfully guides you through not only how to find a home, but how to finance, market, sell, and even invest in real estate online.

With a well-deserved emphasis on selling "For Sale by Owner," the author does not try to make you into a real estate agent. Instead he empowers you with the knowledge necessary to save thousands of dollars in potential commissions. He does this by providing the necessary information and resources for you to make an informed decision. Jack Segner's years of mortgage banking and real estate experience really become evident as he guides you through the daunting task of shopping and eventually applying for a mortgage online. He completely takes the fear out of the entire process.

All in all, a fantastic "how to" book that is actually enjoyable to read, and one that I will refer back to often as a continuing source of information. *Sams Teach Yourself e-Real Estate Today* is destined to be that dog-eared book, full of yellow sticky notes, that is never far from your computer.

Darren Ullmann
Real Estate Guide
About.Com

Acknowledgments

To the professional team at Macmillan USA (Sams Publishing), especially Jeff Schultz, who believed in me and was willing to help promote a first-time author. This book is a team effort and, without the competent support of the editorial staff at Sams, I could not have brought a rough manuscript to an acceptable finished product. While many people contributed to the final product, I alone am responsible for any errors or omissions. My particular views and sometimes acerbic opinions of the real estate and mortgage industries are mine alone and do not necessarily reflect those of the publisher or other contributors.

To my family, especially my wife, Jennifer, and my two oldest boys, John Michael and Robert. You supported this effort and took on the extra burdens of family responsibilities while Dad was glued to the computer. Thank you all again.

To my real estate and mortgage industry friends and colleagues for their input and help. I would like to acknowledge Joel Wilmoth of Realty World Results Plus in Indianapolis who, besides being a good friend, gave valuable advice and counsel, and who continually exemplifies in word and deed what a professional real estate agent should be.

INTRODUCTION

Real Estate and the Internet

Long resisted by the real estate profession, the Internet has become increasingly essential to the efficient marketing of residential real estate. From only about 1,200 sites in 1996 to over 475,000 in 1999, real estate on the Net is exploding. Information is available everywhere, from large national listing sites to smaller regional sites and thousands of individual realtor sites. The problem now is not lack of information and resources but how to find and take advantage of the best information.

This book will be your guide through the maze of information about real estate now available on the Internet. It will teach you how to use the Internet effectively and efficiently to buy, sell, and finance property.

Databases of residential property for sale were once the private domains of Boards of Realtors' Multiple Listing Services (MLS). Virtually every metropolitan area had one or more MLS systems. Access to these systems was restricted to realtors, who acted as gatekeepers of the information about what was for sale. To reach the maximum buyer market, sellers were forced to list their homes with a realtor to be part of the MLS database. This is all changing now, much to the benefit of the homeowner, with the growth of the Internet and the World Wide Web. Some of the results of this dramatic growth are that

- Public access to the MLS systems is now possible on the Internet.

- Listing databases for homeowners wishing to sell their own properties without a realtor's help are proliferating in every market.

- Mortgages are sold online now, and rate information is freely available.

Consumers have more information about all aspects of the real estate transaction than ever before. But the huge volume and unorganized nature of the information make finding exactly what you want difficult and time consuming. This book's intent is to teach you how to successfully exploit the real estate information on the Internet to your advantage.

How This Book Can Help You

If you are facing the daunting array of issues and possibilities involved in buying your first home, or if you are a seasoned homebuyer (or real estate investor) looking to buy, sell, trade up, or relocate, this book will help you understand the myriad of online resources available to you. By learning how real estate resources on the Internet can help optimize your transaction, you will benefit through time and money saved (or profits made) as you sell, buy, and finance your next property.

Organization

The book is organized in four parts and three appendixes. Part I focuses on buying, Part II on selling, Part III on financing, and Part IV on real estate investing. In the appendixes are compilations of recommended sites, a glossary of real estate and mortgage terminology, and information about the companion Web site for this book.

Part I: Using the Internet to Find and Buy a House

In Part I, we cover the basics of finding property on the Internet. With nearly half a million sites related to real estate—and 22,000 of those containing property listings—you need to parse down to the sites that have the best chance of helping you find what you really want. The goal of Part I is to help you find exactly the property you want and can afford to buy.

Part II: Let the Internet Help Sell Your Home

The two chapters of Part II guide you to the best listing sites and teach you how to market and sell your home online yourself. Should you decide to list and sell with a real estate agent, you'll learn how to find a good listing agent and how to help that agent market your property.

Part III: Financing (or Refinancing) Your Home Online

Once you've found your next home, you'll need a mortgage—unless you're one the fortunate 11 percent of homebuyers who pay cash. Most of us will need a mortgage and, in Chapters 7 and 8, we will tour the online lending landscape; find the best loan sites; and learn how to qualify, shop rates, and apply for a mortgage online. Mortgage lending on the Internet is highly competitive; you can find very good deals that can save you up to several thousand dollars on your next mortgage.

Part IV: Use the Internet to Find Bargain and Investment Property

If you are interested in real estate investing, either as a buy-and-hold owner of rental property or as a speculator, Part IV covers the opportunities and resources for investors to be found on the Net. Maybe you want to find a bargain or distressed property to rehabilitate for a personal residence rather than for investment purposes. The information is here for you to take advantage of. Although it is written for the real estate investor, the first time buyer or current homeowner will find valuable information in Chapter 9 of this part of the book.

How to Use This Book

This book is tutorial in nature, but not every reader needs to read the entire book start to finish. (Note: I presuppose a modest level of competence in using the Internet, so there is no "how to use the Internet" instruction.) Here is how I recommend you approach the book, depending on your own requirements as a buyer, seller, or investor.

- **For the First Time Homebuyer:** If you are a first time homebuyer, read all of Part I and all of Part III. Chapter 9 of Part IV is about how to find bargain properties online and could be a valuable resource for you, so read it also. Appendix A contains a glossary of real estate and mortgage terms and will be useful for you to refer to as you read.

- **For the Experienced Homebuyer or Seller:** Experienced homeowners interested in buying should read Part I, skipping Chapter 2, then Part III about financing. Sellers should start with Part II and then read Parts I and III if they are planning to buy again.

- **For the Real Estate Investor:** If you are an experienced real estate investor, read Part IV, starting with Chapter 9 if you are buying; start with Chapter 11 if you have investment property to sell. Parts I and II can be read after Part IV.

The following summary gives a recommended reading plan by type of reader:

Reading Plan

	First Time Homebuyer	Experienced Buyer or Seller	Real Estate Investor
Chapter 1 Overview	Suggested	Optional	Optional
Chapter 2 For first timers	Required	Skip	Skip
Chapter 3 For buyers	Required	Required, if buying	Optional
Chapter 4 Buying from the owner	Required	Optional	Optional
Chapter 5 Selling by the owner	Skip	Required, if selling	Optional
Chapter 6 Selling (with an agent)	Skip	Optional	Skip
Chapter 7 Financing	Required	Suggested	Skip
Chapter 8 Applying online	Required	Optional	Skip
Chapter 9 Finding bargains online	Suggested	Suggested	Required, if buying

	First Time Homebuyer	Experienced Buyer or Seller	Real Estate Investor
Chapter 10 Financing investment property	Skip	Skip	Suggested
Chapter 11 Selling investment property	Skip	Skip	Required, if selling
Appendix A Glossary	Suggested	Optional	Optional
Appendix B Recommended Real Estate Web Sites	Suggested	Suggested	Suggested
Appendix C Using RealEstate-Insider.com	Suggested	Suggested	Suggested

Now that you have an idea how to work through the book according to your personal situation, let's get started.

PART I

Using the Internet to Find and Buy a House

CHAPTER 1

A Brief Overview of Real Estate in a Networked World

As we begin this journey into the world of e-Real Estate, learning how to buy, sell, and finance real estate with the help of the Internet, we need to put this online revolution of electronic commerce in perspective. It will help to understand some history of how real estate has been marketed in the pre-Internet era and just what impact the Internet is having on the industry.

Most people have a sense of how real estate is bought and sold. You see a yard sign or a newspaper ad offering a home for sale. Usually, with a 90 percent or better probability, the seller is an *agent* for the homeowner, a *real estate agent*. You call the number on the sign or in the ad to find out more about the property, since the price and address are not given. Then you begin your involvement with a commissioned salesperson, the dreaded real estate agent.

Perhaps you were interested in buying a home and wanted to know what homes were on the market in a particular area. Your only option in the past was to deal with a real estate agent to have them search the listings (homes for sale) in their proprietary database, the closely guarded MLS, or multiple listing service. That was then, but now the Internet is revolutionizing how real estate is marketed. The goal of this book is to teach you how to benefit from this revolution.

How the Internet Is Changing Real Estate

Today you have many more options to find a home or to sell your home than by calling a real estate agent or real estate office, thanks to the rapid growth of the Internet and the World Wide Web. As recently as the end of 1996, there were only about 1,280 Web sites related to residential real estate on the WWW. Today there are over 475,000 sites, a phenomenal growth rate average of over 190,000 sites per year.

Try It Yourself ▼

Try this query on my favorite search engine, HotBot (*www.hotbot.com*):

1. Go to the advanced search page, select Exact Phrase and English in the first two selection boxes.

2. In the word filter section, select Must Contain and then type this:

    real estate

3. In the remaining drop-down selection boxes, specify Must Not Contain the Words and type this list of words in the additional entry areas (you will have to expand selection boxes with the More Terms option):

    commercial mortgage news software apartments training industry development appraiser trust loan loans mortgages developer mexico canada

    The purpose here is, by exclusion, to find sites in the United States that are related only to residential real estate.

4. Further down on the search page, select Anytime for date published and North America (All) for location/domains, and then select the Top Page radio button to keep multiple pages on the same site from being counted.

▲

When I did this identical query on August 26, 1999, I came up with 475,210 matches. This is neither a perfect search nor a perfect count, but it gives us a sense of how much real estate information is now on the WWW. By comparing the number of hits you receive when you run this query with the elapsed time, you can estimate how quickly real estate information is growing on the Internet.

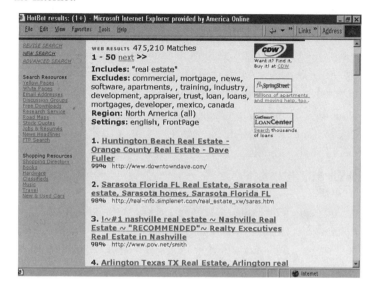

Here are the restricted search results for real estate on HotBot.

If you browse the results of the previous search, you will begin to appreciate the breadth and depth of real estate information now on the Web. One of our challenges in this book is to learn how to parse down this massive amount of information to find just what we want, which is what we will do in Chapter 3, "For Buyers: How to Find Your Dream Home." As you peruse these search results, you'll find that many sites are those of individual brokers and agents, but there are also "for sale by owner" (FSBO) listing sites. What we are seeing is nothing less than a paradigm shift in the way real estate is marketed.

Breaking the Realtor/MLS Monopolies

Thanks to the Internet and the changes taking place in real estate and mortgage finance, the monopolistic practices of the real estate industry are being broken down. In the very recent past (1995), your choices for finding real estate for sale were limited to these venues:

- The real estate section of the newspaper

- *For Sale* signs you might see driving through a target neighborhood

The Paradigm Shift:

A *paradigm* is a model or pattern. What is meant by the phrase *paradigm shift* is this: The conventional pattern of marketing real estate is shifting to a new pattern or model that the Internet makes possible. In the current market, you can make use of online listings and direct marketing of properties by individual sellers or their agents.

- Various free real estate magazines

- A search of the local multiple listing service by a real estate
  agent

These options are still with us, but now we have the Web and
access not only to realty listings, but also to individual for sale by
owner listings, read-only access to MLS systems, and various
national, regional, and local databases of real estate listings.

No longer do the real estate agents have a database monopoly.
You can search just about any MLS system in all 50 states. You
can't list your property for sale on an MLS system without an
agent and a listing agreement, but you can search the marketplace
without having to deal face-to-face with a salesperson.

As an example, try this URL to access the Metropolitan
Indianapolis Board of Realtors (MIBOR) site. This site is available to the public and allows searches of the MLS database:

http://www.mibor.com

From the MIBOR start page, go to PROPERTY and try a search
of Marion County (Indianapolis) to see listings of interest. You
can search for homes by price range and number of bedrooms and
baths. This sample site gives you some but not all the capabilities
of the MLS database.

*Homebuyers and
sellers in
Indianapolis can
use the
Metropolitan
Indianapolis Board
of Realtors
(MIBOR) Web site
to learn about the
local market with-
out first contact-
ing a real estate
agent. Other
metro areas have
similar sites.*

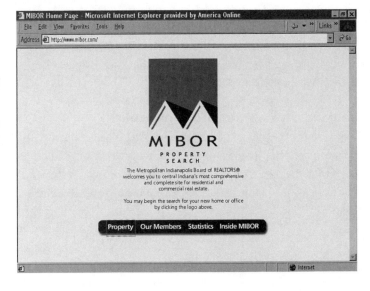

Nonetheless, you can now survey all homes in your price range in a location of interest, without ever contacting a real estate agent. This capability did not exist as recently as 1997.

Some of the most important information contained in the MLS databases is the aggregate data on home sales. When I searched all townships in Marion County in late August 1999 with a query designed to pick up all listings, I found that there were 3,762 homes listed by real estate agents for sale in this central county of the metropolitan Indianapolis market. By going to the STATISTICS page, I also found that for the entire metropolitan area covered by the MIBOR MLS database, a total of 6,935 homes were sold in the second quarter of 1999 (April to June). And, at the end of June, there were still 10,837 active listings (homes on the market). With a little arithmetic, I determined that 70.7 percent of the homes sold in this time period were sold in 60 days or less. This reflects a fairly hot market with real estate agents doing a good job of selling the listed properties.

Never before has this level of detail been available to the general public without contacting a real estate agent. Is this information valuable? You bet it is. If I were going to sell my home in this market by listing it with a real estate agent, do I need to sign a standard 6-month listing agreement? When 70 percent of the market sells in less than 60 days, I would be a fool to let an agent have an exclusive right to market my home for the typical 180-day period. If homes are moving this quickly, I might attempt to sell my home without an agent. Real estate agents no longer have monopolistic control of the market information.

At the end of Chapter 3, you'll find the links to online MLS systems for all 50 states.

Opening Up Access to Financing

A successful real estate broker once told me, "the only thing I really have to offer buyers and sellers is the MLS and access to financing." Real estate agents have long been the gatekeepers of real estate finance through their close relationships with lenders and loan officers. In the past, a prospective homebuyer would invariably rely on the agent's recommendation of a lender or a particular loan officer for a mortgage. Most consumers, assuming

Remember:

In the past, real estate agents have monopolized access to vital local housing market information. This is one way they created a need for their services. With Internet access to MLS systems, you can review and evaluate the same information available to agents and verify their assessments about the market.

the greater expertise of the agent, welcomed this recommendation; most less-sophisticated buyers still routinely take the agent's advice without comparison shopping. This is great for those of us in the mortgage business, because real estate agent referrals are the backbone of most lenders' business.

But the Internet is changing this referral approach to financing. Now, you don't need the agent's advice as much as you did in the pre-Internet days. You are never more than a few mouse clicks away from finding the current mortgage rates for your market area. Online mortgage lenders are featured on most major portal sites and on AOL's Personal Finance channel. You can hardly surf the Net without seeing a banner ad for a mortgage lender.

So although real estate agents may still have cozy relationships with mortgage lenders and loan officers, their advice is subject to review by even the most casual Internet user. Here is a simple test you can do: Call any local real estate office and ask an agent whom he would recommend that you call to get prequalified to buy a home. Be honest and say that you want to do some comparison shopping, but tell the agent that you would appreciate his advice about which mortgage companies to research. Then, with the names of those loan officers in hand, make a few calls and get quotes on current rates for a conventional 30-year fixed rate mortgage. Tell each loan officer that you will be putting 20 percent down and that you will need about a $125,000 mortgage.

After you have a few quotes from local lenders, let's go online and see how your local rates compare. Go to the Bank Rate Monitor site at *www.bankrate.com* by entering this URL: *http://www.bankrate.com/brm/rate/mtg_home.asp*

If this link is broken, go to *www.bankrate.com* and select MORT-GAGES from the links on the side panel of the main page.

From this page—after noticing the average national mortgage rates in the table—select your state from the drop-down selection box and follow the steps on the next page to get individual lender quotes for your city. See how your telephone research compares to this brief survey of online rates. The point of all this is to demonstrate that with one URL entered and four or five mouse clicks, you have a dozen or more current rate quotes from national and local lenders, priced for your market, right in front of you for side-by-side comparison. How long did this online rate survey take, compared to those phone calls? How did your real estate agent's referred lenders compare to your online rate survey? The Internet is truly changing the way we can get information about real estate and mortgage lending. (We will learn in Chapter 7, "Financing Your Dream Home," the best ways to research mortgage rates and lenders.) What you have just done is an example of how the Internet is changing the way entire industries operate. It also brings us to a phenomenon that is accelerating as Internet and electronic commerce grows: the elimination of the middleman (or *middleperson*, to be politically correct).

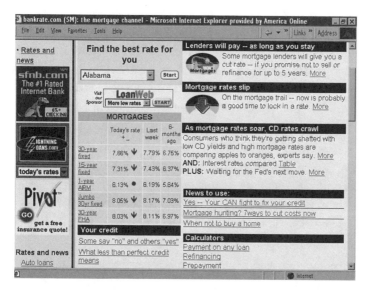

The average national mortgage rates from Bankrate.com do not reflect local market variations, but they do indicate the trend when tracked over time.

The Disintermediation of Brokers, Agents, and Loan Officers

One of the major changes occurring in American business because of the growth of the Internet is the changing role of certain service providers and so-called middlemen. Nowhere has this change been more dramatic than in the stock brokerage industry. Online stock trading and investing, according to industry sources, now accounts for about 25 percent of all stock market volume on the three major exchanges. Even the venerable Merrill Lynch, whose

CEO once stated that online investing over the Internet was not in the best interests of the client, has capitulated and begun offering online trading to its customers, bypassing the traditional broker.

The trend, made possible by the Internet, is for more and more transactions of all types to execute directly between the consumer and the product or service vendor. Dell Computer, for example, is selling over $1,000,000 worth of computers per day directly to end users from its Web site. Dealers and distributors, typical middlemen in the sales process, have been eliminated from this revenue stream along with their profit margins. This direct-to-consumer sales channel is more profitable for Dell and gives the consumer both control of the sales transaction and better pricing.

Direct sales of financial services are also growing. Several estimates agree that online mortgage originations of about 1 percent—or $15 billion of the $1.5 trillion mortgage market—occurred over the Internet in 1998. One forecast for the mortgage industry projects that 25 percent of all mortgage volume will be originated online by 2003. This will be incredible growth—from $15 billion to about $400 billion in 5 years.

What will happen to the mortgage brokers and loan officers who are cut out of this $400 billion worth of transactions? They will be "disintermediated," to use a term that has come into fashion to describe the elimination of the broker/agent middlemen in a transaction. When a consumer can deal directly with a vendor or service provider and eliminate a person or company from the middle of the transaction, two benefits may accrue.

Disintermediation:

When you deal directly with an online vendor, you control the time and place of the transaction, and you may save money by eliminating the middleman.

First, the transaction can be made at a lower cost by eliminating the middleman's margin or commission. Look what has happened with the cost of online stock trading. Trades can be made for as little as $7 per trade. Contrast this with the typical full-service stockbroker, where the same trade could cost $100 or more. Some online mortgage companies are offering flat rate fees or percentage fees that are 50 percent less than traditional mortgage origination costs.

The second benefit is 24/7 (24 hours a day, 7 days a week) access and service. Rather than interrupting your workday to contact a loan officer during regular business hours and only on Monday through Friday, you can use the Net day or night to get mortgage rate quotes, do prequalification calculations, and even complete your loan application online. Only the very best middlemen, whether stock brokers, mortgage brokers, real estate agents, or loan officers, will survive in the long run. Disintermediation will continue as more and more consumers make financial service transactions online at lower cost and with greater convenience.

Fortunately, for real estate brokers and agents, houses still must be physically shown to a prospective buyer, and there are many services the agent provides that cannot be obtained online by a homebuyer. So-called "buyer's agents" (who represent only the buyer in a real estate transaction) will survive, but in smaller numbers than today. The listing agent (who represents the seller and markets the seller's home) will be the target of disintermediation by the inexorable growth of online real estate listing services for owners who want to sell their own homes without the service and cost of an agent.

As the volume of online owner listings on the Internet continues to grow, this marketplace will eventually force changes in the way real estate is marketed by real estate brokers and agents. For the first time, they will have to compete in the home selling and home buying processes on price as well as on service.

We will learn more about these trends as we begin to learn the ins and outs of e-Real Estate.

Real Estate on the Internet

We will be learning about various types of real estate resources on the Net as we work through this book. In the sections that follow, we'll introduce some buying and selling resources and briefly discuss a few mortgage finance options. Finally, to wrap up this overview, we'll look at ways to find and track interest rates.

Types of Buyer Resources

Let's assume that you are a first time homebuyer, or that you currently rent and have no property to sell. You want only to buy a home. What resources are available to help you find that perfect home, and where should your start?

If you know the exact location where you want to buy, then you will want to start with the major real estate listing sites, which may have a good selection of homes in your location of interest. The dominant site for realty listings nationwide is Realtor.com, with over 1.3 million listings as of this writing. It is the "official" site of the National Association of Realtors (NAR). The NAR claims to be the world's largest professional association, with over 720,000 members. A tour of this site is taken at the beginning of Chapter 3.

Next you'll want to search the local real estate agent sites in your chosen location and the local MLS if access to one is available. Finally, you will search the for sale by owner sites. One of the top FSBO sites you'll want to search is Owners.com. To make certain that you've covered all the bases, we'll learn how to find and search the classified homes-for-sale sites.

Home page of the Owners.com listing site. This for sale by owner site has the potential to become the dominant listing service for FSBOs nationwide, in effect becoming the FSBO MLS.

Suppose, however, that you are not sure of the exact location where you will be buying your home. Suppose that you want to research a general area, say the Atlanta metropolitan area. What help can you get online?

There are many city and county information resources on the Web but, like most of the Internet, finding exactly what you want can be frustrating. Here is a quick way to research a location. Go to this URL:

http://www.virtualrelocation.com/index.html

This URL is to the home page of a very useful site for researching a location. From the links on this page, select Best Places to Live. As of August 1999, there were 26 excellent links to all sorts of useful information for homebuyers. You can see where your city of choice ranks in *Money Magazine*'s 300 largest metro areas, based on the magazine's quality-of-life criteria. There are links to every kind of statistical source, from FBI crime statistics to economic data, and even detailed information on specific school districts.

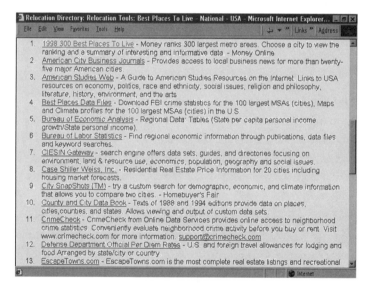

From Virtual relocation.com's site, you can find links to sites for researching the best places to live in the United States.

Some other links you may want to try for location and demographic information are listed in Table 1.1.

Table 1.1: Useful Links for Location Data

URL	Comments
http://usacitylink.com/	Links to city-related sites.
http://govinfo.kerr. orst.edu/usaco-stateis.html	Easy access to census data on U.S. counties.
http://verticals.yahoo.com/ cities/	Comparisons of cities on various criteria.
http://venus.census.gov/ cdrom/lookup/	Access to detailed census data, down to zip code level.
http://homefair.com/home/	Interesting relocation resource but personal info is required to get some reports.
http://govinfo.kerr.orst. edu/sddb-stateis.html	Quick access to school district data.
http://stats.bls.gov/ cpihome.htm	Census lookup for Consumer Price Index (CPI) and other indices. Difficult to use.
http://www.census.gov/ statab/www/	Online access to statistical abstract of the U.S. Excellent for state, county, and MSA data and rankings by data element (such as crime or housing costs).

Listing Resources

If your primary interest at the outset is selling your home, there
are more resources to help you on the Net than you will be able to
use. In Part II, we focus on using the Internet to help sell your
home. Here we will just preview the categories you will work
with later.

Should you decide to use a real estate agent to sell your home,
you will want to list with a top agent who makes good use of the
Internet to give your property maximum exposure. I mentioned
Realtor.com earlier as a buyer resource, but it is also a resource
for you as a seller.

Your most critical task is to select a competent, professional agent
or broker to list your property. You can start your search at the
Realtor.com site by using the Find a Realtor selection and working
your way through a search for several agents to interview. This site
is slow and cumbersome to browse, but it has good content and is
worth a look when you are getting started. Not every agent in your

market area will be found that way. You can also search for individual agents' Web sites, using a restricted search on one of the search engines. You can get some insight into the quality of the agent by the type of information presented. Is he simply hyping past performance (agents love to do this) or does the site reflect a serious attempt to inform you about what advantages the agent has to offer in marketing your home? Develop a short list and then start some diligent comparison shopping.

The most exciting aspect of real estate on the Net is the plethora of resources available to help you sell your own home. A full chapter in this book is devoted to this topic, but here is a preview of what you'll learn.

First, you must determine if you are really in a position to sell your own home. Is there enough time? Are you willing to show the property on demand to prospective buyers? Can you realistically price your home? Do you have the energy, money, and motivation to market your home aggressively, using all types of media? These are some of the questions to answer in your own mind before you become a for sale by owner seller.

Next, you must exploit the best sources on the Net to help you find buyer prospects. The resources you can use include these:

- National FSBO listing sites such as Owners.com

- Local FSBO listing sites in your market area

- Portal sites such as Yahoo!, Excite, AltaVista, AOL, and others

- National and local classified ad sites

The problem is not finding places on the Net to market your property, but finding the sites that are cost effective and give your home maximum exposure. Spend some serious time working through Chapter 5, and you will be rewarded with an effective plan for using the Net as one of the media for marketing your home yourself.

Financing: Mortgage Loans and Rates Online

Getting a mortgage for your home purchase has never been easier than today, because of the dramatic growth of online access to

Shopping for a Real Estate Agent:

We will cover several approaches to shopping for a real estate agent in detail in Chapter 6, "Helping Your Realtor Sell Your Home."

Sell Your Home Yourself:

Chapter 5, "Sell Your Home Yourself and Save Thousands," teaches you how to be a FSBO and use the Net to market your home online.

lenders and information. You can shop nationally, regionally, and locally for a lender. You can do all sorts of mortgage planning and analysis online. You can even apply for your mortgage online and get an approval—*before* you begin shopping for a home.

A Quick Survey on Online Lenders

How many hits would you expect on a search for individual Web sites having to do with mortgages? I found 110,820, using a restrictive search to eliminate duplicate references and irrelevant information. How do we cope with so many sources? In Chapter 7, we will dig into the research needed to find the best source for your mortgage, depending on your particular circumstances and requirements.

The mortgage resources on the Net fall into three broad categories:

- Traditional national mortgage lenders with Web sites, such as Countrywide and Norwest and hundreds more that lend in all or almost all of the 50 states.

- Local and regional lenders, of which there are thousands.

- The new breed of strictly online lenders and brokers, such as E-LOAN, Quicken Mortgage, iOwn.com, Mortgage.com, and many more.

Getting a Mortgage Online:

Chapter 7 surveys the online mortgage world; Chapter 8, "Applying for Your Mortgage Online," guides you through the online application process.

Finding the right lender is no small undertaking; plan to spend some long evenings in front of your computer with this book as your guide through this maze of information.

Monitoring Mortgage Rates

If you're seriously into buying mode for a home, you will want to start monitoring mortgage rates so that you know how to find out quickly what the market is doing and where rates are heading.

Rates change daily, and sometimes even more than once per day. If you have applied for a loan but have not locked in a rate with your lender, then following the market is crucial. A good loan officer will warn you if rates are starting to rise and advise you to lock.

Because mortgage rates correlate closely with U.S. Treasury bond yields, the best way to keep up with rates is to follow the bond market. To get the best and most timely information about bond rates, do what the professionals do: use Bloomberg. This New York–based information service provides online, real-time financial information to the securities industry. Bloomberg dominates the desktops of professional stock and bond traders nationwide. For the investing public, near real-time information on stocks and bonds is available from the Bloomberg Web site.

Go to *www.bloomberg.com* and select U.S. Treasuries from the selection side panel. Scroll down the page to show the Treasury bonds we are interested in most: the 15- and 30-year bonds.

Stocks and Bonds Online:
For daily bond market analyses and excellent historical charts of bond and mortgage rates, go to *www.briefing.com* and check out the U.S. bond market section of this free service.

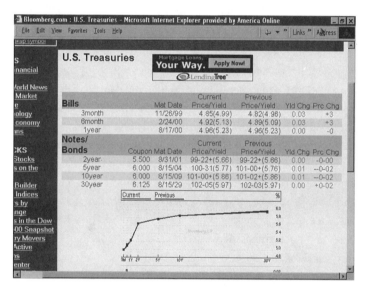

Bond data from Bloomberg.com. Changes in yields on 10-year and 30-year Treasury bonds predict changes in mortgage interest rates.

Under the Bonds heading, look at the 10-year and 30-year bond prices and yields. The last two columns are most important. When you see a price change in red, bonds are selling off in price and yields are rising, as shown in green under Yld Chg to the immediate left. This is what we watch. Mortgages rates track the yield changes in the 10-year bond quite closely. The 30-year yield is a bellwether indicator of long-term interest direction. Both yields move in tandem, but the 30-year bond is more volatile.

When you see changes of 8/32 or more in red under the price change for the 10-year bond or for the 30-year bond, you can be fairly certain that, if the trend continues into the morning of the next trading day when lenders price their loans, rates will be higher, as evidenced by higher discount points. (We'll cover rates and discount points later, so don't worry about the exact meaning now.) Be aware that if bonds begin a downtrend in price, you can expect mortgage rates to rise.

I check Bloomberg several times a day so that I can be on top of rate movement and can advise my customers whether to lock their rates in or to continue floating with the market.

We now know how to follow the bond market sentinel for mortgage rate trends. But where do we find good information about actual mortgage rates?

A site we previewed earlier in the chapter, Bankrate.com, does a thorough job of summarizing average rates nationally and by state. It is worth bookmarking this site so that you can navigate to it easily. But as long as you're going to Bloomberg.com to find out how the bond market is doing, you can quickly and easily get mortgage rates (supplied by Bankrate.com) by selecting Mortgage Rates from the summary table on the right side of the Bloomberg.com home page. You'll have to scroll down the home page a bit to see this link. What you get is a succinctly presented summary of rate information from Bankrate.com. There is a table showing current rates and three graphs showing the past 24 months' trend for the 15-year fixed, the 30-year fixed, and the 1-year adjustable mortgages. This page is a quicker and easier source than going to Bankrate.com for tracking the national averages.

Another good source of rate information is Interest.com, an information site published by Bill Steele, a nationally syndicated mortgage columnist, whose company is called Mortgage Market Information Service. From this site, you can get many rate quotes from lenders in your state by a simple query. You can also subscribe to a free email daily newsletter that Bill Steele publishes after the bond market closes. It is informative but not specific about rates.

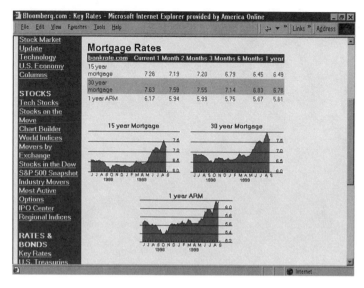

Average mortgage rates from Bloomberg.com. The source of this data is Bank Rate Monitor (www.bankrate.com), but here you get nifty graphs for the most popular mortgage rates.

For quick average rates for your state, go directly to Quicken.com's mortgage rate page with this link:

http://mortgage.quicken.com/Tools/TodaysRates/start.asp

You'll get a simple form to fill out for state and type of mortgage (choose Fixed). Submit the form to get a summary of average rates for your state. Bookmark the resulting page and you can select and refresh it whenever you want to get a quick look at average rates in your state.

Wrapping It Up

This chapter has given you a preview of what you are going to learn about in much more detail and depth as we continue our e-Real Estate education. So far, you've learned how the Internet is changing the way real estate is marketed. You've also learned what some of the buyer and seller resources are, what's available in the way of mortgage lending on the Net, and how to monitor interest rates.

Now it's time to get down to business and find that first home, if you are a first time homebuyer. If you've owned a home before, you can skip Chapter 2 and go straight to Chapter 3 to learn how to find your dream home online.

CHAPTER 2

For First-Time Homebuyers Only

If you have never owned a home, then this chapter is required reading. There is a lot to understand about buying a home and about home ownership in general. This is a case of "what you don't know *can* hurt you." Ignorance is *not* bliss when we are dealing with the single most important financial transaction most people ever make.

Are You Ready for Home Ownership?

The first questions you must answer intelligently and honestly are "Are you ready for home ownership? Do you want the responsibility of the financial obligation of a mortgage at this stage in your life? Are you willing to do the work required to maintain a house and yard? Can you accept the commitment to ownership over the flexibility of renting?"

If you can answer *yes* to each of these questions, you are probably ready for home ownership. If you are unsure about one or more of these questions, you should carefully analyze your personal situation before making the decision to buy a home.

In the sections that follow, we will look at some important facts and issues about home ownership and analyze them in more detail.

Pros and Cons of Owning a Home

There are a number of factors to consider when you are buying a home. Some are objective and some are subjective. The simplest way to organize them is with a decisional balance sheet, or a "pros and cons" list, a methodology proposed over 200 years ago by Benjamin Franklin. In a letter in 1772 to the famous British scientist Joseph Priestly, Ben wrote

> ...my way is to divide half a sheet of paper by a line into two columns; writing over the one *Pro*, and over the other *Con*...I put down under the different heads short hints of the different motives, that at different times occur to me, for or against the measure. When I have thus got them all together in one view, I endeavor to estimate their respective weights, and where I find two, one on each side, that seem equal, I strike them both out. If I find a reason pro equal to some two reasons con, I strike out the three. If I judge some two reasons con, equal to some three reasons pro, I strike out the five; and thus proceeding I find at length where the balance lies...[1]

Let's apply Franklin's balance-sheet approach to the home ownership versus renting decision. Look at Table 2.1.

Table 2.1   Pros and Cons of Home Ownership Versus Renting

PRO	CON
Tax benefit of mortgage interest deduction	Long term financial responsibility of mortgage
Constant, known housing payment; rent could increase	Higher initial cost for mortgage over rent
Control and use of property, no landlord or lease regulations	Restrictive covenants in some developments may limit freedom of use
Safe investment	Illiquid investment
Equity growth over time	Added costs of property taxes and insurance (both can increase)
Price appreciation over time	Price stagnation possible, price declines possible in some markets
Capital gain avoidance, can trade up to more expense home without incurring tax liability	Maintenance responsibilities and costs

1 Quoted in <u>Decision Making</u>, Janis and Mann, 1977, The Free Press, New York, NY

PRO	CON
Pride and status of ownership	More costly to sell and relocate compared to renting
More choices of locations and school districts	Ownership in desired locations may be too costly or unattainable compared to renting
Commitment to and investment in community	Probably fewer amenities compared to renting

How you weight and evaluate each of the pros and cons will determine whether home ownership is right for you at this point in your life. You may value the flexibility of relocating every year or two over settling down in one location and owning a house for three to five years. The greater cost and financial commitment may be big issues to you if you are just starting a new job. Do you want to spend the time, energy, and money to maintain a home? (You might opt for the lower maintenance obligations of a condominium.)

One indisputable fact should be considered and weighed accordingly. The single-family, detached home has been the single most profitable and secure investment for the majority of Americans during the twentieth century. Whether the home will remain the best investment into the twenty-first century remains to be seen. With overbuilding in some markets and supply and demand imbalances in other markets, there is no certainty that the home you purchase today will appreciate reliably and indefinitely into the future. Nevertheless, for most Americans, home ownership represents a store of value and a systematic savings vehicle through equity growth.

Single-Family Detached or Condo

Before analyzing the rent versus buy decision further, we should mention a few facts about condominiums (*condos* for short) as a choice for a first home. In some respects, condos combine the advantages of home ownership with some advantages of renting. You own only the interior of a condominium; the exterior, the land, and common areas are owned by the homeowner's association. With some condo developments, you can get amenities like those found in luxury apartment complexes. You have the tax advantages of home ownership without the burden of exterior and yard maintenance. (You will pay for maintenance and insurance through the homeowners' association dues required with condo ownership, but the maintenance will be contracted out.)

Condos can be ideal for single people and couples without children. They are generally smaller and less expensive to buy initially than a single-family detached home. The biggest negative (and this is not universally true) is that condos are harder to sell, and they appreciate less than single-family detached homes. Personally, I have owned two different condos over the years. One was a personal residence and one was a vacation home. Fortunately, I never had a problem selling and made gains on both. However, I attribute this good experience with condo ownership more to luck than to shrewd investing. We need to consider the economics of home ownership versus renting in greater detail.

Rent-Versus-Buy Analysis

There are online resources to help you analyze the financial side of the rent-versus-buy decision. We will go online shortly and see an example. First, let's be sure to understand some terms we'll be using in our analysis. We will be calculating the total cost of owning or renting over various time frames.

Because there is a higher initial cost of buying, shorter time frames tend to favor renting, but many variables come into play. The investment, or "savings," rate is significant, as is the amount of down payment and the mortgage interest rate. An important concept is the investment rate. If you use $10,000 for a down payment on a home, you don't have that money for other investments. Thus, a proper analysis will consider the savings or investment returns foregone by investing in a home, as well as the estimated price appreciation of the home. The analysis also includes the costs of acquisition of the home (buyer's closing costs) and selling costs (sales commission and seller's closing costs).

Other costs of owning include maintenance, insurance, and property taxes that are not incurred when renting. Because interest on mortgage debt is deductible on federal and state income taxes, tax savings can be obtained for homeowners but not for renters.

If your marginal tax rate is 33 percent, then $10,000 of mortgage interest paid in a year provides a tax savings of $3,333 and costs $6,667, as opposed to $10,000 paid out as rent. Our analysis will consider all costs, tax savings, appreciation, purchase price, rent and estimated increases, down payment, and mortgage interest rate. Assumptions are made about the savings rate, annual price appreciation, and rent increases. The calculations will be made and the total costs of owning and renting compared. By varying the assumptions and time frames, we will get a grasp of how these factors influence the economics of renting and buying.

Economics of Rent Versus Buy

Point your browser to *www.mbaa.org/consumer*, the consumer's page of the Mortgage Bankers Association of America Web site. This site has excellent planning and calculation tools (provided by FinanCenter, Inc.). Note: AOL users can access the same calculators from the Personal Finance real estate channel. From this page, select the calculator icon and you will be taken to the page shown in the following figure.

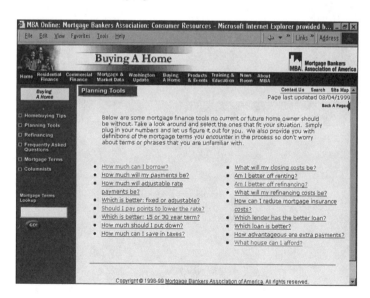

Planning tools available from www.mbaa.org. Each of the underlined questions is a link to a calculator that helps answer the specified planning question.

From this page, select the Am I Better Off Renting? link to get to the calculator. Fill in the calculator form exactly as shown in the following figure (actually, the figure has been "fudged" to show all the fields in the calculator; you'll have to scroll down to access all these fields). Then select the Results tab at the top of the form. The next figure shows the result of this analysis.

Fill in the fields in the www.mbaa.org's Am I Better Off Renting? calculator to get some reliable financial data about renting and owning.

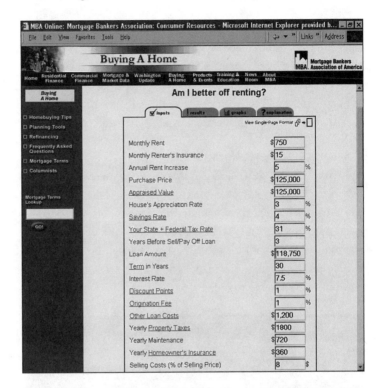

After filling in the calculator fields as shown in the preceding figure, here are some real financial numbers you can mull over when making your decision.

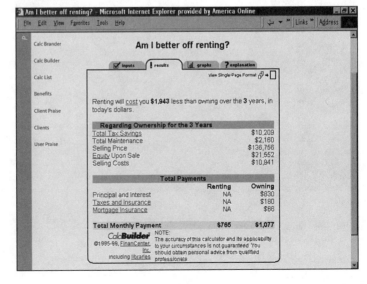

Note that over the 3-year period selected, renting cost $1,943 *less* than buying—even with a minimum 5 percent down payment. Change the period to 5 years, however, and you'll find that buying *saves* $7,285 over renting for the longer period. The graph in the following figure illustrates how buying is more advantageous in the long run.

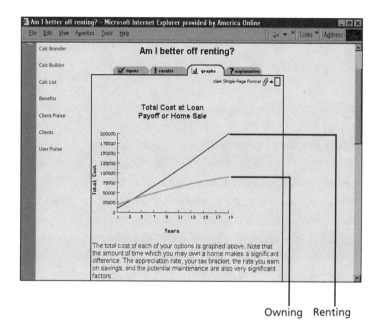

Select the Graphs tab to see a more long-term view of the financial benefits of owning over renting.

It is very illuminating to run this analysis with varying assumptions about the savings rate, appreciation rate, and interest rate. As interest rates rise on mortgages, every thing else being equal, the advantage of buying over renting takes longer to achieve. Likewise, if you increase the savings (or investment) rate, to say 16 percent, you'll find that renting is more advantageous for a longer period, especially if a larger down payment is made.

Try this analysis with factors you think are reasonable for your personal situation, and see what you discover. You may find that if you are planning to move again in less than three years, renting may be a more attractive alternative than buying, at least on a purely economic basis. Over a five-year period or longer, however, buying will usually prove to be much more advantageous.

Your Home as an Investment

The single-family detached home (contrasted with an attached townhome or condominium) has proven to be the best long-term investment for the average American. Because of the steady rise in property values and new construction costs, and because of the very positive tax advantages of home ownership, continuous home ownership is a safe and sure way to invest for the future. Capital gains made on the sale of a primary residence are rolled over, tax-free, into the next home, and at retirement age there is a one-time tax exemption on the final sale of a residence.

Buying a home becomes a savings program because part of each monthly payment is principal repayment that builds *equity* (ownership) in the property. As your home appreciates over the years, your equity increases further. Let's say that you buy a $150,000 home today and you can afford a 15-year mortgage. In 15 years, you will own your home free and clear of any debt, and it will have appreciated, perhaps as much as 75 percent. Therefore, your equity would be $262,500. If you had chosen to rent for those 15 years, you would have no equity other than what you could have saved and invested above your monthly rental payment over that time period—plus, you would still have a monthly housing payment.

Go back to the rent versus buy calculator and see the results of owning a home for 10, 15, 20, and 30 years, compared to renting over the same periods. No matter how conservative your assumptions about appreciation and savings rates, you will find home ownership to be an outstanding long-term investment.

What Can You Afford?

If buying a home is the right decision for you, then what can you buy? How much house can you afford? Mortgage lenders look at your income and obligations to determine what amount they are willing to lend to you. This amount is the amount you are qualified to borrow, based on your qualifying income and debt ratios. You may not want to borrow the maximum you qualify to borrow, but it is useful to know that amount. What then are qualifying income and debt ratios?

Qualifying Income

The income used for qualifying for a mortgage must be *stable* and *continuing*. Lenders have guidelines defining what is meant by stable and continuing. Gross income (before deductions) from your salaried or hourly paid job is considered qualifying income if you have worked in the same field for at least two years.

If you are self employed or receive more than 25 percent of your income from commissions or bonuses, your qualifying income must be determined from the previous two years of Federal tax returns. This presents a dilemma, because it is the net profit reported on your Federal Schedule C or your adjusted gross income that is used, after averaging over two years and year-to-date of the current year. If you write off many expenses, you may have a problem showing enough qualifying income.

Some income that you might think would be counted is acceptable only under certain constraints. For example, income from a part-time job you started just several months ago would not be counted, unless you had a history of working both full-time and part-time jobs. Overtime, unless there is a two-year history, is generally not counted. Child support received can be used if there is documented evidence of regular payments.

When we go online shortly to prequalify, and you are asked to enter your monthly income, keep this information in mind and don't overstate your income.

Debt Ratios

Lenders look at how much installment and revolving debt you pay each month. These debt payments, combined with the proposed housing payment, divided by your monthly qualifying income equal your total debt-to-income ratio. This ratio should not exceed 41 percent for FHA loans and 36 to 38 percent for conventional loans. There are circumstances in which these ratios can be higher, but these are the conservative numbers.

Your proposed monthly housing cost, including your mortgage payment, taxes, homeowner's insurance, and any mortgage insurance, when divided by your monthly income, should not exceed 29 percent for FHA loans and 28 percent for conventional loans.

FHA Loans:

FHA loans have more lenient underwriting standards than conventional loans. Made by private lenders but insured against default by HUD, FHA loans are intended to expand homeownership among lower income borrowers and minorities. Mortgage insurance is paid to HUD by the FHA borrower monthly and as a one-time fee added to the loan.

Conventional Loans:

Conventional (or conforming) loans are those that conform to the strict underwriting guidelines of the agencies (such as Fannie Mae and Freddie Mac) that purchase these loans from mortgage lenders. Conventional loans require private mortgage insurance if less than a 20 percent down payment is made, with some exceptions.

Again, these ratios can be stretched if there are compensating factors, such as a large down payment or substantial savings.

Lenders look at all the risk factors when underwriting a loan. If your situation appears more risky to an underwriter, you can expect the ratio guidelines to be more closely followed. If you have fewer risk factors, you may be allowed higher ratios. Table 2.2 shows a few of the factors that affect risk in the loan approval process.

Table 2.2   Risk Factors That Affect Qualifying Ratios

Factor	More Risk	Less Risk
Down Payment	Low 3–5%	High > 20%
Cash Reserves	None or < 2 months' housing payments	Significant savings, > 6 months' paments
Job Stability	Frequent job changes	> 2 years on same job
Prior Housing	First-time buyer	Previous homeowner
Debts	High debt burden	Low indebtedness
Income Stability	Self-employed or commission income only	Salaried or wage earner

Many first-time homebuyers have more rather than fewer risk factors relating to income, debts, and job stability. If you fall into the More Risk category, you can expect less flexibility in exceeding the traditional debt ratios.

However, let's not be pessimistic. Let's move ahead to prequalifying yourself to see how much mortgage debt and housing cost you can afford.

Prequalify Yourself Online

Most of the online lenders as well as sites such as the Mortgage Bankers Association site we saw earlier have prequalifying calculators we can use. One of the best is found at *www.financenter. com/homes_page.html*.

We will select How Much Can I Borrow? to reach the online form. The top part of this form is displayed in the following figure, with some sample values already entered.

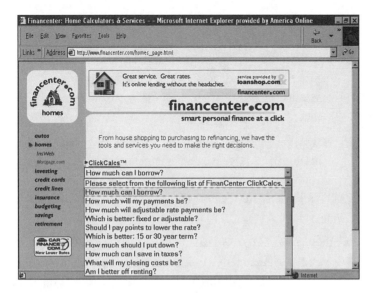

Prequalifying calculator selection from Financenter.com.

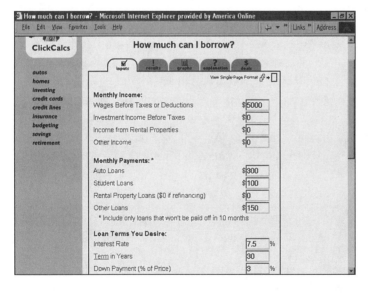

Use Financenter. com's How Much Can I Borrow? calculator to determine the mortgage amount you can qualify for.

A Prequalifying Scenario

1. In the fields on the How Much Can I Borrow? calculator, enter the combined qualifying income of one or more borrowers as a monthly (gross) figure. In this example, we use $5,000/month as income.

▼ **Try It Yourself**

2. Under Monthly Payments, enter some payment amounts. Although the form asks for loans, you can enter any type of installment or revolving (credit card, department store) payments. Be sure that you include all minimum required payments. Do *not* enter utility or insurance monthly payments.

3. Next, enter an interest rate, term, and down payment (as a percentage). Use 3 percent as the minimum down payment (or any other amount you choose). When we get to the results, your down payment entry, plus 5, 10, and 20 percent down payment options, will be automatically calculated for you.

4. Further down the form (scroll down), you'll enter the estimated annual property taxes and insurance premium you might be paying. For this example, annual taxes of $1,800 and insurance of $480 were used. Because your total housing payment including principal and interest, taxes, insurance, and mortgage insurance is used in the ratio calculation, it is very important to estimate the property tax and insurance premium. The monthly mortgage insurance premium (for down payments less than 20 percent) will be calculated for you. (Don't worry if you have no clue about what all this means at this point. You will get a thorough review of mortgage lending basics later, in Chapter 7, "Financing Your Dream Home.") For now, we just want to get an idea of how much we can borrow and what factors affect the amount.

5. Click the Results tab to go to the completed prequalification calculation page, shown in the following figure.

Down Payment Percentages:

The down payment percentage you enter on this calculator is always a percent of the price of the house. The calculator works backward from the debt and income ratios to arrive at a maximum mortgage amount and then calculates the house price based on the down payment percentage.

Looking at this figure, we see that there are two estimates of the prequalifying scenario, one conservative and the other aggressive. Remember the earlier discussion of risk factors in loan approval? The aggressive scenario assumes lower risk and higher ratios. For most first-time homebuyers, however, the conservative scenario will be more appropriate; we will focus on it here. Notice that, depending on your down payment amount, the house price could vary from a low of $144,730 to a high of $189,489—with the same monthly outlay of $1,250 per month at our assumed 7.5 percent mortgage interest rate.

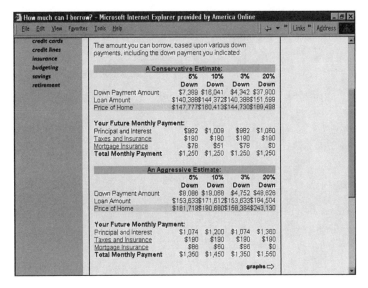

Sample prequalifying results. Notice that with a fixed housing payment, you always qualify for a more expensive home by making a larger down payment.

How did the calculator arrive at $1,250 as the allowable monthly housing payment? It used the two ratios we've discussed: 28 percent of income for housing and 36 percent for housing and other debts combined. In our example, 28 percent of the $5,000 monthly income is $1,400. If we had debts of only $400, we could use this higher housing payment; but because 36 percent of $5,000 is $1,800, and we have $550 of debt, we are constrained by this ratio to a housing payment of $1,250 ($1,800 minus $550) rather than $1,400. As you can see, the ratios are used together to determine our maximum allowable housing payment.

It is crucially important for you to understand the impact of debt on qualifying for a mortgage. If we had only $400 per month of debt payments, as opposed to $550 in our example, we could qualify for houses priced from $165,211 to $216,314. This additional $150 of debt per month has cost us about $21,000 of additional qualifying mortgage amount. This is because at a mortgage rate of 7.5 percent, each $7 per month pays for $1,000 of mortgage; we have $150 of monthly payments disallowed by exceeding the ratio for total debt, so our allowed maximum mortgage is reduced by $21,000.

This next figure, which was generated from the Graphs tab of our calculator form, shows the impact of monthly debt on mortgage amount.

Remember:

If your ability to qualify is constrained by debt, reducing debt is a much more powerful factor than increasing income. It would take $415 more income per month to offset $150 per month of debt. A $150 reduction in monthly debt payments allows you to qualify for $21,000 more in mortgage amount.

The effect of monthly debt on qualifying mortgage amount. As you see here, each $200 of monthly debt reduces the loan amount you qualify for by about $28,000.

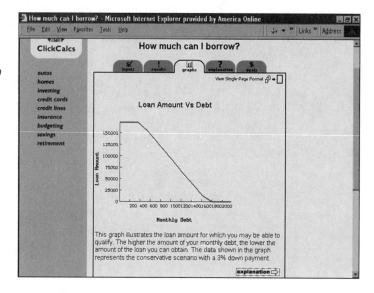

You should now use the online prequalifying calculator at *www.financenter.com/homes_pages.html* to run your own prequalification scenarios, with particular emphasis on what would happen if you reduced your monthly debt. That extra car, boat, or motorcycle payment could make the difference in your first home being just average or truly special. After you have determined on your own what you can qualify for, let's confirm your figures by prequalifying with an online lender.

Use the Online Lenders to Prequalify

If you would like to experiment with getting prequalified by an online lender, try one or more of these sites:

- *www.eloan.com*

- *www.mortgage.com*

- *www.quicken.com*

- *www.loanworks.com*

See how your qualifying compares with the online calculator results. Then go to *www.loanz.com*.

The www.loanz.com home page. This site uses current rates in the pre-qualifying calculations and offers free qualifying software you can download.

At Loanz.Com, try the Buyer Qualifier function, which uses their best current rates for two different loans to qualify you. Then go back to the home page and download the free POWERHOUSE software. This useful program for homebuyers includes a mortgage qualifying section you can use to analyze your particular situation by running all manner of "what if" calculations quickly and easily. You'll have to register this program before you can use it by calling a toll-free number, but it is a free package for unlimited use. You will find some useful tutorials on the home buying process, loan comparison features, a rent versus buy analysis, and other features. This is not the ultimate home buying software, but it is freeware, well worth the time to download, install, and explore.

All this analysis is just an interesting exercise, however, if you don't have money saved for a down payment on your new home. What can you do if you are short of cash for that all-important down payment?

Down Payment Is the Biggest Hurdle

Buying a home is a major financial decision, and it takes a significant amount of money, unless you qualify for 100 percent financing and the seller pays all or most of your closing costs. If you do not have savings or other liquid assets such as stocks or bonds to turn into cash for your down payment and closing costs, what are your alternatives?

Where to Get the Down Payment

There are several ways to get down payment funds that are acceptable to mortgage lenders, depending on the type of loan program used:

- *Gifts from family members or non-profit organizations.* FHA allows all of the required 3 percent down payment to be a gift. Conventional lenders allow gifts of down payment and closing cost funds, if the borrower contributes at least 5 percent. (If the donor gives 20 percent, the borrower does not have to make the 5 percent down payment.)

- *Unsecured loans* from employers or disinterested third parties, a charitable organization, church, or government entity (not from the seller, builder, or real estate agent).

- *Loans secured by financial assets*, such as life insurance or mutual funds or other stocks or bonds.

- *Loan from the seller* (seller financing).

- *Funds from the fair market sale of assets.* Cars, boats, antiques, collections, or any other tangible asset you own can be sold in a documented, arms-length transaction to a third party (not to your mother, brother, or friend) to raise money for your down payment.

- *Cash value* from surrendered life insurance policies.

- For FHA borrowers, a *gift from the Nehemiah Foundation* may be used for the down payment. (See the section on assistance programs later in this chapter.)

- For certain conventional loans, a *credit card cash advance* can be used for the down payment.

- *State and local community housing grants* and assistance programs can fund down payments, either through gifts or loans. (See the section on assistance programs, later in this chapter.)

As you can see from this list, there are many ways to get the money for a down payment. Closing costs, which can run as much as 3 or 4 percent of the purchase price, can be paid by the sources already listed or by the seller, the lender (through something called *rebate* or *premium pricing*), or a combination of seller and lender contributions. Can we avoid making a down payment at all? The answer is *maybe*, depending on your circumstances and preferences.

One Hundred Percent Financing Options

There are two superb ways to buy a home with no down payment, or with what we call *100 percent financing*:

- If you are a military veteran with at least 90 days active duty or six years in the Reserves, you are probably eligible for a VA (Veterans Administration) loan. VA loans can be for 100 percent of the purchase price of a home. Either you or the seller will have to pay closing costs, because they cannot be financed in the loan. A VA loan does not require monthly mortgage insurance and has a competitive interest rate with conventional loans. You can borrow up to $203,000.

- If you have modest income and are willing to buy in a designated rural area and meet some additional constraints, a Rural Housing Development (RHD) loan is just the ticket. Formerly called Farmers Home Administration loans (FmHA), this loan is similar to a VA loan. You get 100 percent financing and pay no monthly mortgage insurance. Even better than a VA loan is your ability to finance all costs into the RHD loan. The intent of the program is to lend to people who buy in rural areas and have no financial capacity to get a conventional or FHA loan. Certain metropolitan areas and counties are excluded entirely from this program, as are towns with populations of 50,000 or more. There are property requirements to meet (in particular, some strict thermal standards), but this is an ideal way for some first-time homebuyers to buy a home with literally no out-of-pocket money.

If you don't qualify for these two 100 percent loan programs, you still have plenty of options.

There are many so-called non-conforming 100 percent loan programs. These loans have strict credit requirements and carry higher-than-normal interest rates (2 to 4 percent higher, for example). A typical program would allow you (or the seller) to pay closing costs, which would be the only required funds for the purchase. This higher-interest, 100 percent loan should not be your first choice, but if nothing else will work, you may want to investigate these programs. (We cover how to do this in Chapter 7.)

Some of the best 100 percent options or down payment solutions may be found right in your own community, and many are accessible online.

Assistance Programs: Find Them Online

In many urban areas, you will find a state, city, or county "housing authority" whose mission is to help foster homeownership for low- or modest-income families or individuals. In my state, there is the Indiana Housing Finance Authority (IHFA), which issues and sells bonds to subsidize low-to-moderate-income borrowers with below market interest rates and down payment assistance.

A list of every state housing agency can be found online at this site:

http://mortgage101.com/pg00252.htm

This list has addresses and telephone numbers, but no Web site URLs or email addresses. To find the Web site of a housing agency in your community or state (if one exists), you will need to search your state's Web site. Table 2.3 lists all 50 states and their Web site addresses.

Table 2.3   State Web Site Addresses

Web Site URL	State
www.legislature.state.al.us	Alabama
www.state.ak.us	Alaska
www.azleg.state.az.us	Arizona
www.state.ar.us	Arkansas
www.state.ca.us	California
www.state.co.us	Colorado
www.state.ct.us	Connecticut
www.state.de.us	Delaware

Web Site URL	State
www.dos.state.fl.us/fgils	Florida
www.state.ga.us	Georgia
www.hawaii.gov	Hawaii
www.state.id.us	Idaho
www.state.il.us	Illinois
www.state.in.us	Indiana
www.state.ia.us	Iowa
www.ink.org	Kansas
www.state.ky.us	Kentucky
www.state.la.us	Louisiana
www.state.me.us	Maine
www.mec.state.md.us	Maryland
www.state.ma.us	Massachusetts
www.migov.state.mi.us	Michigan
www.state.mn.us	Minnesota
www.state.ms.us	Mississippi
www.state.mo.us	Missouri
www.mt.gov	Montana
www.state.ne.us	Nebraska
www.state.nv.us	Nevada
www.state.nh.us	New Hampshire
www.state.nj.us	New Jersey
www.state.nm.us	New Mexico
www.state.ny.us	New York
www.sips.state.nc.us	North Carolina
www.state.nd.us	North Dakota
www.state.oh.us	Ohio
www.oklaosf.state.ok.us	Oklahoma
www.state.or.us	Oregon
www.state.pa.us	Pennsylvania
www.info.state.ri.us	Rhode Island
www.lpitr.state.sc.us	South Carolina
www.state.sd.us	South Dakota
www.state.tn.us	Tennessee
www.state.tx.us	Texas
www.state.ut.us	Utah

continues

Table 2.3   Continued

Web Site URL	State
www.state.vt.us	Vermont
http://dit1.state.va.us	Virginia
www.wa.gov	Washington
www.state.wv.us	West Virginia
www.state.wi.us	Wisconsin
www.state.wy.us	Wyoming

A useful exercise for you to do now is to search your state's Web site to find all the housing agencies. Check out the down payment assistance programs. There is one program I found in Indiana that gives you $2 for every $1 you save for a down payment. Other programs make interest-free loans for down payment assistance, and some offer subsidized interest rates. You will find that most of these state, city, and county programs have income limits and other conditions. They are generally not available for poor credit risk borrowers.

There is another way to get a gift for your down payment, rather than dealing with the state and county housing authorities. The most exciting program for you to consider if you are going to use an FHA loan and need down payment assistance is the Nehemiah gift program. You can get all the details at *www.nehemiahprogram.org*. The following figure shows the home page for this site.

The Nehemiah Program home page. This non-profit organization provides down payment gifts for FHA borrowers.

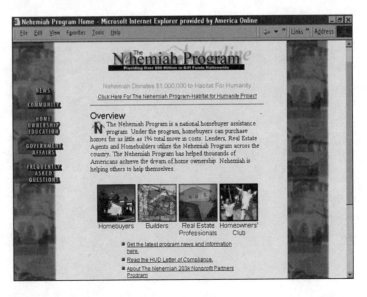

Here is how it works: A seller agrees to participate in the
Nehemiah Program. You offer to purchase with an FHA loan
using the Nehemiah Program gift for your required 3 percent
down payment. The seller (a new home builder, an FSBO, or any
seller of an existing home) agrees to pay the Nehemiah Program a
4 percent service fee at closing and signs an agreement to that
effect. Based on that agreement and your FHA-approved loan,
Nehemiah remits a gift of 3 percent of the purchase price to you
at closing to cover your down payment, required with an FHA
loan.

Some organization you probably never heard of is willing to give
you money to buy a home! Is this a great country or what? It's
legal, ethical, and there are no hidden strings attached. Over
23,000 such gifts have been made. There are a couple of conditions to this program that complicate the transaction, but which
are easy to meet:

1. The seller must provide a 2-year roof warranty.

2. The seller must provide a 1-year home warranty.

3. The borrower (you) must complete a home ownership coun-
   seling course.

4. The borrower (you again) must have 1 percent of the purchase price in reserve. This can be any financial asset,
   another gift, an IRA or 401K, the cash value of life insurance, savings bonds, or any other liquid asset. The money is
   not required to be spent on closing costs or prepaid expenses
   (these can be financed into an FHA loan). You just have to
   prove you have 1 percent of the purchase price in some form.

If you and the seller can meet these four conditions, the
Nehemiah Foundation will happily send you several thousand
dollars for the down payment on your first home. What a deal.
So, what's the catch? There is no catch—you can get this money,
providing that your credit is acceptable, which brings us to the
final topic of this chapter.

Warning:
As of October 1999,
HUD has proposed
new rules that could
disallow the
Nehemiah FHA gift
program and any
others like it. If disal-
lowed, there will be
a six-month phase-
out period. You may
have to hurry to
take advantage of
this program in the
year 2000.

How Is Your Credit? (Hurdle #2)

Mortgage lenders make lending decisions based on an analysis of your income, assets, job and income stability, property value and, most importantly, your credit history. *All the other factors will be ignored if your credit history is unsatisfactory.* You could have twice the price of the house deposited in your bank account, make a $500,000 per year salary, and still be denied for a 95 percent conventional mortgage on a $100,000 home purchase.

Your Credit History Is Critical

Most first-time homebuyers (and some experienced buyers) simply do not understand how critical credit history is to the mortgage industry. Even though the loan is secured by a home, lenders do not want to foreclose and will go to great lengths to avoid originating loans that may result in foreclosure or delinquency. Furthermore, since 99.9 percent of all mortgage lenders are resellers of mortgage loans in the secondary market (to agencies such as Fannie Mae and Freddie Mac, as described in the glossary to this book), their loans must conform to the credit quality guidelines of these agencies if they are to be sold.

FHA has somewhat more lenient credit guidelines than the agencies; FHA exists to expand home ownership among those who cannot qualify for conventional loans. A major growth industry in mortgage lending, called *subprime lending*, has developed to serve consumers whose credit history is not otherwise acceptable.

What Is Subprime Lending?

If your credit category is not "prime," or the top grade that lenders call "A credit," you may be funded by a so-called "subprime lender." These lenders specialize in lower credit grade (B, C, and D) or subprime borrowers.

What is acceptable credit? In the old days (pre-1995), if you had a credit history such as that shown in Table 2.4, never had a bankruptcy, had no judgments or collections, and had at least four sources of credit, you were deemed credit worthy for conventional mortgage lending. That was before the mortgage industry embraced credit scores as the primary underwriting guideline.

Table 2.4   Acceptable Traditional Credit History

Type of Credit Obligation	Time Frame of Credit Performance		
	Last 3 Months	Last 12 Months	Last 24 Months
HOUSING (mortgage or rent)	No late payments	No late payments	No more than 1 30-day late, no 60-day or later

Type of Credit Obligation	Time Frame of Credit Performance		
	Last 3 Months	Last 12 Months	Last 24 Months
INSTALLMENT ACCOUNTS (car loan)	No late payments	No more than 1 30-day late; no 60-day or later	No more than 2 30-day or 1 60-day; no 90-day or later
REVOLVING ACCOUNTS (credit cards, dept. store)	No late payments	No more than 2 30-day late; no 60-day or later	Same as for installment accounts

There are other considerations for satisfactory credit history and performance. Remember our discussion earlier about job and income stability, assets, and debt ratios? These are equally important for loan approval. When underwriters review a loan application, with the borrower's documentation of income, job history, financial assets, a satisfactory credit report, the property appraisal, and shoe size, they can still find ways to deny the loan. If everything is in order, including satisfactory credit performance per Table 2.4, the denial will usually be based on low credit scores. How can this be? What are *credit scores*, and why are they so critical?

All About Your Credit Scores

The mortgage industry uses a credit scoring methodology developed by Fair, Isaac and Company, Inc. (FICO), a credit research and consulting firm. Your credit history and performance, as maintained on the databases of the three major credit bureaus—Equifax, Trans Union, and Experian (formerly TRW)—are run through the Fair, Isaac software model. The output is a credit score, generically called a FICO score. This score is a figure of merit, which ranges from about 450 to 850, and is alleged to be highly predictive of future credit worthiness. This score is crucially important for you to understand. It can help you get the best possible conforming loan, or it can relegate you to the underworld of mortgage lending, the dreaded subprime category. Credit scoring is a mixed blessing. It can help or hurt, and you need to understand it.

How Can You Get Your Credit Score?

You can't! The bureaus (Equifax, et al.) will not provide your score in a consumer credit report. You can get your FICO score only by having a lender request it and then sharing the information with you. *Never deal with a lender who refuses to show you your credit report and scores.*

What is the magic score? It is 620. A score below 620 will almost guarantee that you will *not* get a conforming loan; you'll need an FHA or subprime loan.

Here is the bottom line on credit scores:

FICO Score	Mortgage Credit Decision
Over 800	Top of the line; loan officers will beg for your business, so shop them ruthlessly and demand rate concessions.
720-799	Slam dunk; approval by automated underwriting; denials are rare.
660-719	Approval generally assured, unless you have skeletons in your credit closet (like a bankruptcy).
620-659	Very careful scrutiny by human underwriters, usually not automatic or computerized approval; may not get the terms you want (such as 3 percent down).
619 and below	You are toast; FHA or subprime is your destiny.

To learn more about credit scoring and whether Fair, Isaac and Company is really fair to the borrowing public, check out these sites:

- *www.fairisaac.com*

  Get the party line from the source. Go to the consumer info section and read all about credit scorings benefits and how you can improve your credit profile and score.

- *www.creditinfocenter.com*

  Consumer advocate site with very interesting inside information on credit scoring, plus valuable self-help information on credit repair.

- *http://members.aol.com/victcrdrpt/Score.html*

  The dark side of credit scoring is covered in this personal site about victims of credit scoring. This site contains the following news story of how Federal Reserve Board member Lawrence B. Lindsey was denied a Visa card in 1995:

A salary of $123,000 and a seat on the Board of the Federal Reserve wasn't enough to convince computers at the Bank of New York to grant Lawrence B. Lindsey a Visa card. Published reports indicate the credit scoring program rejected the application because the applicant had 8 reports issued in the last year. Both Toys "R" Us and Bank of New York issued statements regretting the incident and offering Mr. Lindsey a card. No mention was made in either statement of the millions of ordinary citizens who are victimized the same way each year. Mr. Lindsey has been a vocal critic of credit scoring systems for some time. The Associated Press quotes him as saying "If human beings are taken out of the loop, some rationality and common sense is lost in the process."

The purpose of all this is not to terrify you about credit scoring but to make you an informed credit consumer. You can't do much in the short run about your credit score. Some of the things you can do to maximize your credit score over time simply have to do with responsible credit use and behavior. Here are some basic guidelines:

- Avoid derogatory credit events such as collections and judgments. Refusing to pay a disputed debt on principle may make you feel righteous, but the damage done to your credit file is not worth the seven years of grief this adverse history will cause you. (Seven years is how long adverse information remains on your file; bankruptcy is reported for 10 years.)

- Use some revolving credit (2 to 4 credit card and retail accounts in all), but keep your balances well below credit limits. Pay on time, always.

- Have an installment loan (a car or personal loan), but pay it on time.

- Do not allow routine inquiries into your credit file. Never let a car dealer run your credit unless you have already decided to buy.

- Avoid excessive credit use, and do not borrow from finance companies. Don't apply for credit cards by mail to get low introductory teaser interest rates or to see how large a credit limit you can get.

- Close unused accounts.

- Never, ever get 30 or 60 days late on your mortgage or rent. Housing payment performance is critical.

Fair, Isaac does not reveal the exact methodology it uses to create the FICO score. And while there is no law or regulation to prevent you from having access to your score, you can't get it from the credit bureaus or from credit card issuers. When you apply for a mortgage, your lender will pull a credit report with scores (with your written permission). Because this is such an important issue, make certain your lender will share your report and scores with you. *Don't do business with any lender that says he can't show you your credit report or credit scores.*

What you can do on your own to manage your credit file and get your credit report (you can get it online) is our final topic for this chapter.

Online Credit Reports and Services

The first step in understanding your credit situation is to get a copy of your credit report from each of the major repositories (Equifax, Trans Union, and Experian). You can go directly to the Web sites of these credit behemoths and request your report for $8 each (in most states). Alternatively, you can use one of the online credit services such as *www.icreditreport.com*. This online credit report service will deliver a single report online in a few seconds. You can also get a merged report from all three bureaus. Note that you will not get credit scores in any of these reports.

After you have your credit report, you may need to take action to remove any errors or disputed information. There are many resources on the Net to help you with this process. Some are free, but most charge a fee. You should be wary of so-called "credit repair" services. Most of what can be done to repair your credit file you can do yourself, with some time and effort. You should not need to pay hundreds of dollars to some company to mail a few letters on your behalf. This is definitely a do-it-yourself project.

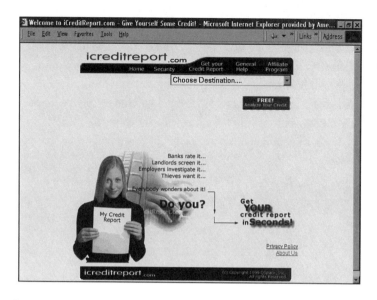

Get your credit report online from icredit report.com.

First, you should understand your legal rights when dealing with creditors and credit bureaus. Go to *www.ftc.gov/os/statutes/ fcra.htm* to get a copy of the Fair Credit Reporting Act. Review §611, "Procedure in case of disputed accuracy," to understand the process for getting information corrected. The bureaus themselves can be helpful online—but with information only. You can't take action from their sites:

- *www.equifax.com*

- *www.experian.com*

- *www.transunion.com*

You can get help and consumer information about credit repair from these sites:

- *http://personalcredit.about.com*

- *www.creditinfocenter.com*

Wrapping It Up

We have come a long way in this chapter. You have learned whether you should buy a home, how to prequalify for a mortgage, and how to calculate the amount you can afford to spend on your first home. You know ways to get your down payment you didn't know before. You have learned a lot about credit files, credit scoring, and credit bureaus. All of this is important, but not much fun.

Now for the fun stuff. In the next chapter, we go house hunting on the Internet.

CHAPTER 3

For Buyers: How to Find Your Dream Home

In this chapter, we will begin our online search for that perfect next home. (If you have never owned a home, you may want to review Chapter 2, "For First-Time Homebuyers Only," before continuing here.) To facilitate your learning the basics of online real estate, we will start with a quick tour online, then visit some of the major realtor listing sites.

Are Homebuyers Using the Internet?

In a July 1999 study released by the National Association of Realtors (NAR), a May 1999 survey of homebuyers showed that 23 percent had searched for their homes online. This is up from 2 percent in 1995. Additionally, 58 percent of those surveyed said online searching was extremely or very valuable. NAR's listing site, Realtor.com, claims to get *90 million* hits per month. That's a lot of homebuyers surfing, wouldn't you agree?

After you are familiar with these listing sites, we will master the efficient use of search engines and local MLS (multiple listing service) sites to make sure that we've covered every possible online realtor listing source for your home search. When you have finished working through this chapter and the next, where we cover the For Sale By Owner (FSBO) online listing sites, you will know how to find a property that meets your exact criteria, if it exists on the Internet.

Finding Listed Properties Online

Let's begin with a quick tour of some of the resources on the Net that are available to you as you begin your search. As mentioned in Chapter 1, "A Brief Overview of Real Estate in a Networked World," there are two main categories of real estate listings on the Net. First and most plentiful are the listings of realtors. Less numerous and more difficult to find are the FSBO listings.

What You'll Learn in This Chapter:

▶ How to use the Internet to look for listed properties

▶ How to find the major listing sites

▶ How to take advantage of the power of technology and take a "virtual tour" of a listed property

▶ Whether or not you should use portal sites as a resource

▶ How to access a multiple listing service state by state

Generally speaking, these two categories are mutually exclusive
and must be searched separately.

We will begin with Realtor.com. This site is the official site of the
National Association of Realtors, which claims to have 1.2 million listings online. It is certainly a worthwhile starting point. Not
every MLS listing from your market area will be here, but this
site should definitely be searched.

To start the tour, go online and access the URL
http://www.realtor.com. From the opening page, use the Find a
Home tab, which is the same link as the Find Your Dream Home
link. This link opens the location map and search page.

For this example, we will use my hometown and search by zip
code. You can substitute your own town or city of choice. If you
click a state on the state map, you get another screen that lets you
select a city; then a further refinement by county, township, or
area is offered. It takes three more screens to get to the final
search screen, shown in the next figure. If we use a shortcut on
the first page and enter the zip code for the area we want to
search and then click the Continue button, we can get to the following screen much faster. Note that you can also do a search by
city name and specify a radius but, because I know the zip code,
it is more efficient to use it.

*The Realtor.com
home page is
where to start
your search of
over a million
listings.*

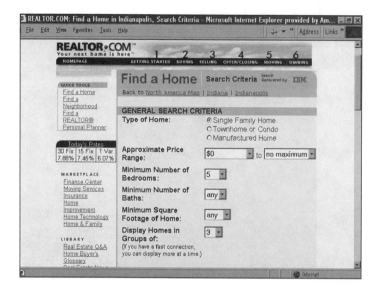

Only part of the Realtor.com search form is shown. Scroll down for more preferences that can be selected to order your results.

On the General Search Criteria screen, we enter the criteria we want for our search. Because I have a large family, I want five bedrooms. Price is always a concern, but I don't want to limit my search on the low end or high end since that could exclude a bargain property or just slightly exceed my upper limit. For example, if I put $195,000 as my upper limit (the maximum I want to pay), I would exclude all prices above that amount. My dream home might be listed for $197,500 (and could possibly be negotiated down), but I wouldn't find it if I limited the price. Leave the defaults in the form except for bedrooms, which we set to five.

Now scroll down to the Other Preferences section of this form and check any features of the property you want to see. I like older homes, so I checked Age 75+ Years. Whatever is checked here does not restrict your search. It just orders your results by the features selected. The Find Homes button at the bottom of the form gives us the results of this search in my hometown (listed by realtors), with older homes shown first, as shown in the following figure.

Remember:

Use the preferences section of the search form to order your results by features you're looking for, such as lot size, age of home, or amenities (such as a swimming pool).

This search resulted in six hits. The first property listing shown is an older home, just what I like. Note that no address is given. This is so that you have to contact the realtor to find out.

Search results for
five-bedroom
homes in zip code
46122. The listings
are ordered with
the older homes
shown first
because of the
preferences
selected in the
search form.

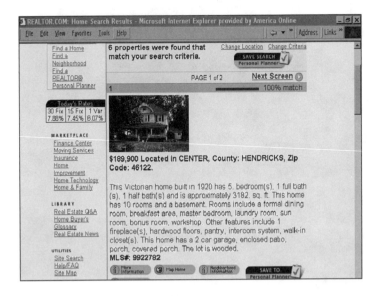

Search results for five-bedroom homes in zip code 46122. The listings are ordered with the older homes shown first because of the preferences selected in the search form.

But notice the selection buttons below the MLS number. The Map
Home button presents a very detailed map of the area, with a little
graphic pushpin at the approximate street address of the listing.
By looking at this map, I could identify exactly where this home
is (about four blocks from my current home). Click the More
Information button to get a larger picture and much more detail
from the MLS listing information, such as room dimensions,
types of rooms, amenities, special features, school district, and
more.

Try your own search, using either city and state criteria or the
state and county maps. After you're finished exploring, we'll visit
some of the other major listing sites.

Visit the Major Listing Sites

We will continue our house hunt by visiting and searching four of
the major listing sites and one hybrid site. If you use these sites in
addition to Realtor.com, you will have access to over 3,000,000
active realtor listings. This is a reasonably efficient way to survey
the market in your desired location. Let's work through all the
sites with the same requirements: Assume that you just got a new
high-tech job with a company in Marietta, Georgia, a suburban
city in northwestern metropolitan Atlanta.

HomeSeekers.com

HomeSeekers.com is second only to Realtor.com in number of listings, claiming it has more than 680,000. It is a somewhat cumbersome site to use, but it is a must-search site because of the number of listings and the probable non-duplication with other realtor listing sites.

Go to *www.homeseekers.com*, enter **marietta** in the city search box, and click Go.

You will have to drill down through two more pages—one to resolve the city (because there is a Marietta in Mississippi and Pennsylvania as well as in Georgia) and then one useless screen on which you simply select Search. (Remember, I said this site was cumbersome.) But now we are at the search page shown in the following figure, which is an excellent page. Notice that, by each city in the scroll box in the lower-right corner, the number of listings is shown in parentheses. Our target city of Marietta has 133 listings.

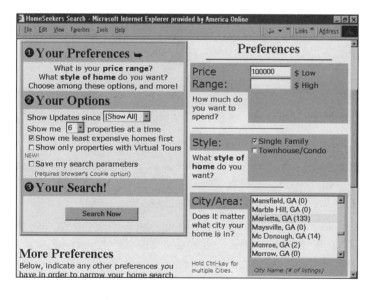

Here's the search page from HomeSeekers.com. Note that the number of listings in each city is shown next to the city's name.

Now fill in a minimum price of $100,000 to eliminate the really low-price properties and select Single Family and nothing else under Preferences. Because this site, awkward as it is to navigate, is fairly fast, we will not restrict our search further but will

browse the results. After submitting this form, we are rewarded
with a hit count of 123 and a neat presentation of listings with
thumbnail photos, which we can expand by clicking the price or
the picture. When this is done, we get the listing agent's name
and more details, including the address. If we click the address,
we get a nice location map generated by MapQuest.

*The results of a
search on
HomeSeekers.com.
The thumbnail
pictures make
the search more
efficient.*

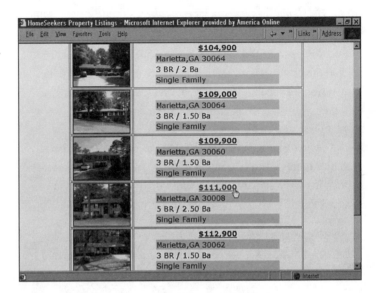

This site has been productive, but let's see what Microsoft has to
offer with its entry in the cyber real estate arena.

HomeAdvisor

HomeAdvisor is Microsoft's effort at a real estate listing site, and
it claims to have over 500,000 listings. Let's see how we do as we
continue to search for a home in Marietta, Georgia.

On the *www.homeadvisor.com* opening page, click the Homes
image in the upper-left corner. You will be asked to download a
plug-in to implement the search engine. (This is Microsoft, so
nothing is easy.) To avoid the download, you can use the zip code
search (if you know the zip code you want). Just for fun, let's go
ahead and do the download, which is fairly quick and painless.

After the download, you will need to work through several
options to restrict your search. You are guided step-by-step on the

various pages. If your parameters are restrictive enough, you will get a results page similar to the one in the following figure. But if your search is not restrictive enough and you get more than 300 hits, Microsoft (authoritarian as ever) makes you go back and further restrict your search until you have fewer than 300. Only then do you get a display.

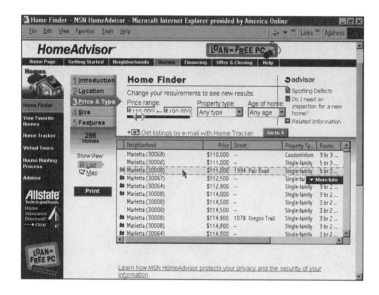

Here are the search results from HomeAdvisor. If you get more than 300 hits, you have to restrict your search further or nothing is shown.

In this results screen, notice that I got 266 hits after restricting the price range to between $110,000 and $190,000. This is an unfortunate search implementation for such a major listing site, and it can be quite frustrating to use. Nonetheless, the results are worth the irritation. The listing information is comprehensive. Double-click a line item to get expanded information and a picture. A location map is also available with one additional click.

As you might expect from Microsoft, HomeAdvisor is comprehensive and feature rich but somewhat difficult to use. Still, this site is a necessary stop on your home search journey.

CyberHomes.com

Our next stop is at CyberHomes.com, another major listing site, claiming to have over 650,000 listings. CyberHomes.com is owned and operated by Moore Data Management Services, a provider of real estate technology for multiple listing services.

This site provides access to realtor listings from local MLS systems and is comprehensive in coverage for the participating locations. To continue looking for a home in Marietta, we find by using a criteria search for homes in the over-$110,000 range that there are over 250 listings. A line item report gives us 25 listings per page; we can expand to a detailed listing with a photo by selecting the MLS number hyperlink.

This site offers several powerful and useful features. The mapping capability is superb, allowing you to select one or more homes to position on a map of the area that can be zoomed down to street level. Then you can specify that schools be shown on the map. From the line item page, I selected the five-bedroom, $111,000 home we found in this and previous searches and mapped it with the schools shown. The next figure shows the result.

A map with the selected property and school location shown from CyberHomes.com.

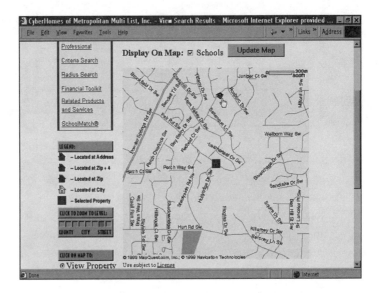

Notice that the map has a scale shown; with it we can estimate that the school is less than a mile from the home we selected. But what kind of school is it? The map display allows us to click the school icon and get a summary report about the school district and the specific school. I found that the school shown is in the Cobb County school district and that it is Hollydale Elementary, which has an enrolment of 720. The address and telephone number of the school are also given. There are also options on the displayed page (not shown here) to let me order detailed reports online or by mail for a fee ($9.95 and $19.95).

If you have children, finding a home within an acceptable school district is usually a major concern. CyberHome.com also has a SchoolMatch function (see the selection list at the top-left of the preceding figure). This link will list all the schools, public and private, in the area of interest. You may find your home through some other site, but CyberHome.com is worth a visit if only for the powerful school location mapping capabilities.

Now let's move on to our last realtor-listing site.

Homes.com™

One of the oldest companies in the online real estate service business is Homes.com, which started offering online services in 1992. It is part of PCL Media, Inc., which publishes and franchises the well-known *Homes & Land* real estate magazine. You have probably seen this magazine in racks at supermarkets or in real estate offices. Advertising is solicited from realtors in each local franchisee's territory.

Their Web site at *www.homes.com* has about 300,000 listings but is less comprehensive than the other sites we've discussed that draw from MLS systems. This site is still useful and rounds out our tour of the realtor listing sites. Using our previous criteria, I found 277 homes to browse in the Marietta area. The line item presentation suffers from not identifying which listings have photos. You have to click the listing to get a detailed report like the one shown in the next figure.

There are several features here of interest. Free reports are offered from the listing display. However, only the School report is online and does not require the input of personal information. The Property and Neighborhood reports require your contact information and will result in the information being passed to the listing agent for the property, who will invariably call you. Be aware of this if you order these reports.

Something's Missing:
Interestingly, when I displayed the five-bedroom, $111,000 home found previously in our searches, Homes.com showed no picture, yet the other sites did have pictures of this home.

A detailed listing display from Homes.com.

One additional feature of this site is the ability to identify child-care providers in the area. This service is provided to Homes.com by CareGuide (*www.careguide.net*), a useful site and worth checking out. CareGuide has a great database of childcare provider information at a useful level of detail.

Although it was not the best search site for our purposes, Homes.com is a useful stop along the way to finding your dream home. Is there an easier way than going through each major site with the same search?

A Listing Search for Other Realtor Sites

One of the sites we will be covering in detail in the financing part of this book is called iOwn.com, a major mortgage-lending site on the Net. It has more to offer than mortgages—it has one of the best search engines for finding realtor listings and For Sale By Owner listings under its Search for a Home feature. Bypass all the introductory pages and go directly to the HomeScout search page at iOwn.com by entering this URL:

http://homescout.iown.com/scripts/ListingSearch.dll/Search

If we now enter on this page the same criteria for our Marietta location as we did in the two previous searches, we get truly interesting results, as you can see in the next figure.

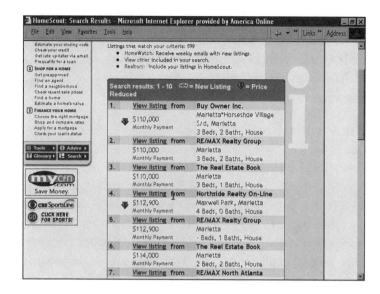

Results from a multiple site search by iOwn.com. This search produced many more properties by combining results from local realtor sites as well as from major listing sites.

First of all, we have 599 hits—almost twice what we got on our earlier searches. In addition, we have a combination of realtor listings and For Sale By Owner listings. iOwn.com pulls data from multiple sources, including two major FSBO sites, Owners.com and Buy Owner (which are covered later in this chapter). There are also listings from individual realtor sites and other listing sites. Here is a list of major sources that iOwn searches and then combines the results:

- Owners.com (*www.owners.com*)

- Buy Owner (*www.buyowner.com*)

- iOwn Realtor Center (*www.iown.com*)

- The Real Estate Book (*www.treb.com/default.htm*)

- New Homes Direct (*www.newhomesdirect.com*)

- Individual Realtor Sites

This combined search capability is extremely valuable, as indicated by the greater number of hits received than in any of our earlier searches. However, it is not an all-inclusive search. Remember the five-bedroom, $111,000 home we found previously? It was not found in the search by iOwn. This fact emphasizes the need to use multiple sites for your searches and not rely on a single site, even if it is more convenient.

We have completed our tour of the realtor listing sites and learned how to use them. Now let's take a break (because this is one of the longest chapters in the book). Come back with a hot or cold adult beverage, and we will continue by looking at a fascinating new technology.

Take a Virtual Tour

One of the most exciting developments in online real estate is *virtual tour* technology. It is in its infancy now but will grow rapidly as the two major players compete for market share in the real estate listing support market. The companies involved are Interactive Pictures (*www.ipix.com*) and bamboo.com (*www.bamboo.com*). Why the funky "bamboo" name? The company claims that all the relevant short names were taken, so they picked a distinctive name. bamboo.com went public with an initial public offering of stock in August 1999 and raised over $28 million. This war chest of capital may help it become the dominant firm in this business.

What is virtual tour technology and what does it do for you, the homebuyer? The technology provides panoramic photography of a home's exterior and significant interior rooms (kitchen, living room, master bedroom, and so on). The companies in this business are selling the videography services for about $100 per listing. The target market is realtors who want to enhance their online listings with dynamite visuals. It appears that FSBOs are being excluded by bamboo.com and that only realtors can use their service. Competition will end this monopolistic practice in the near future.

For now, you can take a virtual tour of a few properties whose listing agents have embraced this technology. You can bet this will grow rapidly to the point where buyers will not bother looking at listings that don't include virtual tours. Let's take a virtual tour now.

Try It Yourself ▼

1. Go to *www.bamboo.com*; from the home page, select Take a Tour to get to the sample tour page shown in the following figure. It takes a moment for the 360-degree panoramic image to load. What you see first is an exterior image of the

property that automatically pans 360 degrees to give you a complete picture of the home and its surrounding area.

2. There are five interior views. You may start out with one scene of the living room.

3. Visit each interior area with the panoramic views. You get a virtual walk-through of the home. Here we are seeing the real power of the Internet as a visual marketing tool for home sellers and buyers. And we got to see this home without ever getting in the realtor's car!

With bamboo.com, you get 360-degree surveys of the exterior of the house and several of the main rooms inside.

Will this "virtual tour" idea take off and be available on every listing? I don't think so. Its initial use will be for marketing upscale properties, primarily for properties listed by realtors. The technology is not being targeted to individual owners. You can see the logic here: If every homeowner could use this outstanding marketing tool, the vendors would have a hard sell trying to overcome realtor's objections. If this unique technology is available only to realtors, it helps them list and sell homes. If it is available to every home seller, it dilutes the realtors' marketing advantage. Until competition forces the two major vendors to seek out the FSBO market, and until prices come down, primarily realtor-listed properties will have virtual tour technology.

The second vendor in this virtual tour technology is Interactive Pictures Corporation (IPIX). They do more than real estate imaging and have interesting technology you can check out at *www.ipix.com.*

Try It Yourself ▼

1. From the IPIX home page, select the real estate virtual tour image, then select Take a Tour from the next page.

2. Select one of the sample tours; the tour image will begin to load in a new browser window.

3. When the image loads into the new window, you can control the panning and zooming of the image with your mouse.

▲

This is great stuff. Interactive Pictures Corporation does not restrict sales of their image technology, so it eventually may be found on some of the FSBO sites we will be discussing later.

A sample virtual home tour from IPIX. Unlike bamboo.com, IPIX does not limit the use of its technology to only realtors.

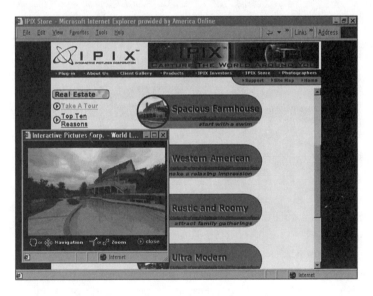

Should You Use the Portal Sites?

What about using the well-known "portal" sites as a quick and easy way to search for your dream home? The major portals, in no particular order, are AOL, AltaVista, Yahoo!, Excite, Lycos, and Netcenter. One of these might be your start page at your ISP.

You would think that with millions of visits per day by Internet users, these sites would be prime real estate listing sites. But they are not. Don't waste your time trying to sort down to the real estate information with any of these. The exception is Yahoo!, which has a fair collection of links to real estate resources.

You will be disappointed if you use the other portal sites as a starting point for searching for home listings. You will end up at Realtor.com, which you already know how to use.

What the portal sites can be useful for is finding homes for sale in classified ads (discussed in Chapter 4, "How to Find the Perfect FSBO Property"). My advice is to use your time searching the sites we learn about here; don't bother with the portal sites.

State-by-State MLS Access

Earlier in this chapter, we covered in some depth the ways to find realtor-listed properties nationwide. What may be helpful for you in certain markets, however, is to go directly to the MLS service in your area of interest. In this section, you learn how to find links to all state, regional, and local MLS systems that have online searchable databases accessible by the public.

Some states have several MLS services that cover groups of counties. Every major metropolitan market is served by one or more MLS system. For instance, the Atlanta metro market has two MLS systems, with limited duplication of listings between the two. To fully search the Atlanta area, you would need to search both systems.

Not every MLS system is accessible over the Internet, but eventually all systems will be. To search within a particular state, you should run these three searches on Yahoo!, replacing the *state* with your state's name:

"multiple listing service" +state –commercial -rental

"board of realtors" +state

"association of realtors" +state

These searches will ensure that you find the relevant MLS sites in your state.

Remember:
This book has a companion Web site that can help you get to the recommended sites. *www.realestate insider.com* provides a helpful way to link to the various sites covered in this book.

FYI:
For your convenience, a complete and up-to-date list of publicly accessible MLS systems is maintained at *www.realestate insider.com*.

Wrapping It Up

At this point, you should be familiar with the following information:

- How to use Realtor.com to find realtor listings nationwide

- How to find other major listing sites to search

- What virtual tour technology is

- How to find MLS listing systems in your state

So far, we have learned how to exhaustively search the major realtor listing sites, but how are we going to find those elusive "for sale by owner" properties? Let's find out in Chapter 4.

CHAPTER 4

How to Find the Perfect FSBO Property

What You'll Learn in This Chapter:

▶ How to find FSBO properties using the best FSBO listing sites

▶ How to use search engine techniques to find properties online

▶ How to search local classified ads online

Unlike the realtor- and MLS-based listing sites, there is no dominant listing site for FSBOs. This will eventually change; one day, there will be a site or sites with a million owner listings online. Until a dominant site develops, the online FSBO market remains a victim of fragmentation. There are hundreds of FSBO listing sites but none has enough listings or traffic from buyers to produce results and grow based on performance. The Net will remain only one way to market property, but over 23 percent of homebuyers are now using the Net to search for homes.

The situation is a bit analogous to the era when there was no Multiple Listing Service for realtors; each real estate office had its own listings, and there was no central repository to search to find all the homes for sale in a given market. Right now, there are a few national FSBO sites and many local and regional ones. What will probably happen is that increasing competition from FSBOs marketing their properties on the Internet will eventually drive down realtor commissions. Once commissions are low enough, owners will choose the convenience of listing with a realtor rather than attempt to do their own marketing.

What are some of the best ways now to find FSBO properties? We must review the major national FSBO sites and then try to find good regional or local sites serving a particular market.

Best National FSBO Sites

There are four major FSBO sites with nationwide listings, although not all 50 states are necessarily represented in every site. We will start with the largest and most elaborate of the national FSBO sites.

A National FSBO "MLS"?

Owners.com may well become the first national equivalent to an MLS for FSBOs. If its growth continues and sellers get results from listing on the site, in a year or two we might just see a revolution in the way real estate is marketed. Stay tuned.

Owners.com

The Owners.com site is by far the largest FSBO site on the Net, with thousands of listings across all 50 states. It got its start back in 1995 (which makes it a senior citizen in Internet years), and it has grown to be the dominant national FSBO site. Go to *www.owners.com*, select Search for Homes, and set up a query for Marietta, Georgia, with homes between $110,000 and $190,000 (the same restrictions we use on Microsoft's HomeAdvisor realtor site earlier and on some of our other searches in Chapter 3).

This search yields 64 properties for sale by owner within our price limits. (Note: If no upper price limit is entered, 122 properties are found.) Recall that when we searched HomeAdvisor with the same price range parameters, we retrieved 266 realtor listings. This means that at least 20 percent of the homes for sale in Marietta are offered by owners. This can be confirmed by recalling that when we did the iOwn search that retrieved realtor listings and for sale by owner listings together, we found 599 properties over $110,000. You can see that 122 is about 20 percent of 599, so it does appear that the FSBO segment of the market in Marietta is about 20 percent.

Owners.com property search results for FSBO listings using our sample query. Note that fewer properties are found than when we searched the realtor sites in Chapter 3.

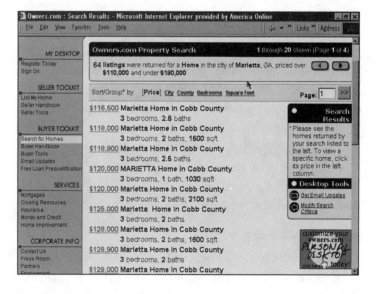

Because it is doubtful that Owners.com captures every online FSBO listing in a market, the actual percentage of FSBOs in a given market is probably higher than 20 percent. This is significant for us because if this number is 20 percent and growing, we want to be sure to reliably reach this market segment in our home search.

I ran some additional searches for five of the larger metropolitan markets to see how many listings were currently on Owners.com. Table 4.1 shows what I found.

Table 4.1   Search Results for Owners.com FSBO Listings in Major Markets

Metro Area	FSBOs >$110K	Entire State's FSBO Listings	
Atlanta	1,230	Georgia	1,718
Boston	503	Massachusetts	650
Chicago	449	Illinois	672
Dallas-Ft. Worth	531	Texas	2,060
Los Angeles	401	California	1,653
Total	**3,114**	**Total**	**6,753**

Clearly, Owners.com should be a primary search location whenever we search for homes. But there are other important national FSBO sites to consider.

Buyowner.com

Buyowner.com is an excellent FSBO site, but it is difficult to determine the total listings available because of the requirement to search by city or county. No state level search is possible. This is not a real problem, because we are always going to search at the city or county level anyway. The opening screen of this very well-implemented site appears in the following figure.

When we use the same search in Buyowner.com as we used in Owners.com, we get 64 hits for the $110,000–$190,000 range and 85 for the above $110,000 search. This compares to 64 and 122, respectively, for Owners.com. The completed search page is shown in the following figure. Notice the thumbnail pictures next to each listing summary. This is a much better presentation than the line item list of Owners.com presents, but it takes longer to scroll through.

FYI:
A 1997 nationwide study done for the National Association of Realtors found that 13 percent of homes were sold by owners without the help of a real estate agent. My personal opinion is that FSBO sales today are about 20 percent of the national market—and growing.

The www.buy owner.com home page; you must search by city or county rather than at the state level, but this is not a disadvantage.

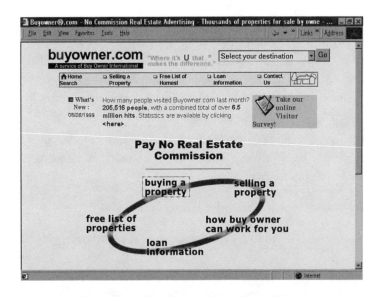

The result page from a Buyowner.com search example. The hit counts compare favorably with that of Owners.com.

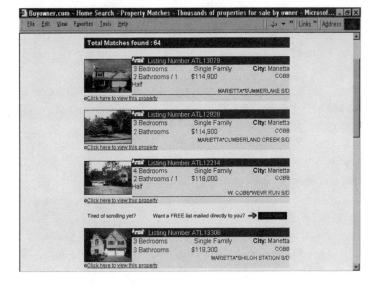

What is truly interesting about the comparison of searches between Owners.com and Buyowner.com is that there appears to be very little duplication of the listings. This tells us that we should not rely on just one national site to search for FSBOs. We must go to each one and perform the identical query.

Byowner

Byowner.com is a no-frills site but one that seems to have plenty of listings. When our sample query for homes priced from $110,000 to $190,000 in Marietta, Georgia, was run, there were 101 line item listings. Unfortunately, the information available is bare bones; although the site supports pictures, on the sample query none of the listings had pictures. The following figure shows one of the listings.

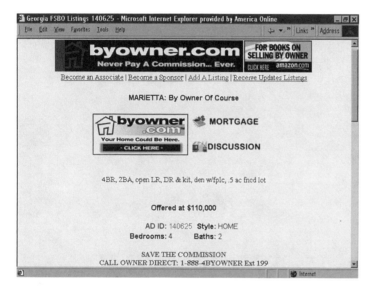

Here's an example of a FSBO listing on Byowner.com. This site protects the seller's privacy at the inconvenience of the buyer.

The toll-free number at the bottom of the screen (the same number was on every listing) gives a recorded message stating that you should leave a number to have the owner call back or you could email a request to be contacted by the owner. This is awkward and inconvenient for you as a homebuyer, but it provides privacy protection for the seller. Privacy can be very important for some sellers, who may not want their personal information (name, address, and telephone number) on the Internet for the world to see.

Byowner.com should rank last on your list of sites to search, but you should still consider it, because it might produce listings not to be found elsewhere.

Inconvenient, But...

With not much information available in the listing, no picture, no address, and no way to easily contact the owner directly, Byowner.com is not as useful as we would like. However, because it protects a seller's privacy, it may be the only place some sellers consider listing.

By Owner Online

Our final national FSBO site to consider is By Owner Online, found at *www.by-owner-ol.com*. This site has nationwide listings but is based in Orlando, Florida, and has a strong presence in the Florida FSBO market with about 1,800 listings. Its coverage of markets other than the Southeast and Midwest is limited. Nonetheless, this site has excellent listing presentations. The sample query we have been using to compare FSBO sites produced 47 listings for our target location. The search parameters do not permit specifying an exact price range. You have to select from predefined ranges (such as 101–125 or 176–200), but you can leave the price parameter blank and pull up all properties in the city or county selected. The first page of our sample query is shown in the next figure.

A listing summary page from www.by-owner-ol.com. This well-developed site has many useful features for buyers, such as email notification and a direct link to school information.

Each listing summary shown provides price, subdivision name, and owner's name and telephone number. The address is not provided. When the listing is expanded by selecting the View Property Description link, a detailed description and a photo appear. Within the listing description, hyperlinks to additional photos of specific areas of the property may be provided. An owner could put a link to another Web page with more information within the descriptive text.

This site provides another very useful feature. You can request a weekly email update of listings that meet your specific query. So, as listings of interest to you are added to the system, you will be notified by email each week.

Another convenient feature of this site is a link to school district information. From a menu bar on the property listing, you can select School Info and be taken to the county school information provided at *www.theschoolreport.com*. This site offers summary school district information for the county where the property is located. You can also submit a request for a very detailed 6-page comparative report on three districts; the report is delivered online after you enter your personal data and agree to receive information from an advertising sponsor.

Strong in the Southeast:

By Owner Online, in addition to being an overall excellent FSBO site, is particularly strong in the Southeast, especially in Florida. In my opinion, this site ranks just below Owners.com as a top FSBO site.

All things considered, this site should definitely be included as a priority in your quest to find for-sale-by-owner properties.

Local FSBO Sites May Be Your Best Source

One thing is clear from our review and testing of the national FSBO listing sites: No single site has every listing in a given location. In some markets, local and regional FSBO sites have grown to provide significant coverage of specific markets.

If you were in, or moving to, the Indianapolis area, for example, you would benefit from using *www.IndyFSBO.com*, a local site that covers the Indianapolis metro area. Finding the best local FSBO sites is a difficult and time-consuming process. One approach is through carefully crafted searches using the major search engines. Another way is to go to the regional area of Yahoo! and search for "for sale by owner" within a specified state. This approach yields many sites and Web pages, which, with some luck and effort, may get you that local FSBO listing site with a good selection of properties.

We will cover the efficient use of search engines later in this chapter and delineate the best search techniques for finding properties that meet your specifications, regardless of the type of listing.

There is one shortcut you can try in your effort to find a local FSBO site. Go to *www.fsboguide.com* to see a link page that has links for all 50 states. The individual state information, when

selected, may or may not give you a decent list of FSBO sites for
your state. You'll have to try it for your state and see what local
FSBO sites are listed.

The Classifieds: Not to Be Overlooked

Because there are still a number of free and low cost classified
advertising sites on the Internet, we must not overlook these as a
source for finding homes for sale. Before the ascendance of the
major listing sites on the WWW, classified ads were a popular
medium for home seller advertising. This is less the case now but,
in an effort to exhaust the possibilities, we should at least search a
couple of the major classified ad sites, starting with Yahoo!.

Yahoo! offers free classified ads; the real estate ads can be found
at this URL:

http://classifieds.yahoo.com/residential.html

From here, you can search by state and city. This is fast and easy
to do, but the results are predominately duplicates of the
Owners.com listings.

Another choice for finding classified real estate ads is on America
Online's ClassifiedPlus service. You do not have to be an AOL
subscriber to access the classifieds. Simply go to this URL:

http://classifiedplus.aol.com

From the main page, select the Real Estate heading; on the next
page, select Search, found under Private Home Sales. The Search
screen will let you specify state, city, and other search parameters.
Because classified advertising is declining in popularity on the
Net, don't expect to find many listings this way. What you need to
do is go to the original source of classified advertising, the news-
papers.

At some point, any home seller who is serious about selling a
home, without exception, will advertise in the Sunday classifieds
of the local newspaper. Even if the owner is promoting his property on every possible FSBO site on the Web, he will still advertise in the local newspaper's Sunday real estate section. So how
do you find the ad? The Newspaper Association of America has
made it simple and easy. They have a Web site that lets you find

any newspaper that has searchable online classifieds. This is one
of the most useful sites on the Internet. Go to this URL:

http://www.realfind.com

If this site fails for any reason, use this URL:

http://www.bonafideclassified.com

From the search page, you choose a state and a city or newspaper
name (if you know it). Alternatively, you can just enter the state
and browse all the newspaper sites in the state. The resulting
search page lets you choose a newspaper in the area of your
interest and then work with that paper's online classified system.

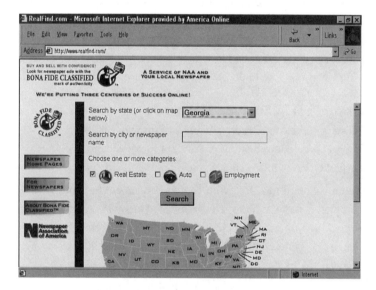

*The Newspaper
Association of
America has
made it easy to
search for homes
in the online
classified ads of
almost any news-
paper in the
country.*

This is a powerful and important capability for you to use on a
weekly basis to find FSBO ads when they first appear. Most
sellers will advertise for four to six weeks in the classifieds
before getting discouraged and listing with a real estate agent.
You want to find these ephemeral ads by searching each Sunday's
real estate classifieds in the appropriate newspaper for your target
location.

By using the online newspaper classifieds, you will be certain to
find properties not found anywhere else on the Internet. The Net-
savvy home sellers will use both the Internet and the newspaper,

but *all* home sellers, at some point, run ads in the local newspaper. Your weekly task, once you have identified your target city and its newspaper, is to search the online classifieds to check for newly advertised properties. I am not a gambler, but I'm willing to bet that just this information alone—how to find online classified ads in any newspaper in America—is worth the price of this book.

Finding Your Needle in the Listing Haystack

If you are an experienced Net user, you've probably been frustrated more than a few times with the overwhelming volume of information you find every time you use a search engine.

The challenge is to find what you want without having to wade through thousands of hits from your queries. This is especially difficult with real estate; in the next sections, we'll spend some effort learning how to do better searches for property.

Using Search Engines Effectively

Mastering the use of search engines to find your home on the Internet is a requirement if you are not lucky enough to find that perfect home with the sites and techniques already covered.

You must learn to search with enough refinement in your search parameters to get a reasonable number of hits without excluding something important. But let's face it: If your search gets more than a few hundred hits, are you really going to look at each one?

FYI:

In this section, we abandon this chapter's FSBO orientation for a moment. We will use the search engines to find property based on *property specifications* rather than *type of listing*.

We will use the major search engines and search with the same query to demonstrate some of the challenges of using direct search engine queries to find a specific property.

Table 4.2 shows the results of using the search specification *home sale marietta georgia* in the main search window of the eight most popular search engines. This, of course, is an unrefined, "quick and dirty" search.

Table 4.2   Hit Count by Search Engine

Search Engine	Hits
Yahoo!	2,442
AltaVista	12,995

Search Engine	Hits
HotBot	1,470
Excite	1,674,867
InfoSeek	13,484,522
WebCrawler	101,371
Lycos	Unknown

Obviously, these results are not very helpful in this form. We must use some additional search techniques to refine our search.

How to Narrow Your Search Without Missing Anything

We want to refine, or narrow, our search for homes for sale in our target location, but we don't want to miss anything by being too restrictive. If we condition our search on each search engine by simply requiring that each word in our simple query appear in the Web page by adding the Boolean *AND* between each word, to require all the words to appear (or the equivalent, depending on the search engine), then our results are narrowed but still include some irrelevant pages. The number of hits is much more manageable, as can be seen in Table 4.3.

Table 4.3   Hit Counts with a Restrictive Search

Search Engine	Simple Search	Restricted Search
Yahoo!	2,442	2,442
AltaVista	12,995	3,043
HotBot	1,470	730
Excite	1,674,867	1,148
InfoSeek	13,484,522	9
WebCrawler	101,371	103
Lycos	Unknown	>400

We have narrowed our results but still have a more inclusive search than we can reasonably review. How can we be more restrictive but still not be too exclusive? Read on!

Finding Only What You Really Want

If you know what you want in a home, you can further restrict your searches without being overly exclusive. Suppose that your home really must have four bedrooms and a basement. (You want to be able to send the kids downstairs so that you and your spouse can have some peace and quiet upstairs.) You can condition your search to find only those properties that have both of these requirements. To see what happens, let's try it with one of the search engines we just used. Enter this more precise specification on Yahoo!:

georgia +marietta +home +sale +basement +4

This request is for those Web pages that have all six terms included on each page; the result is 205 hits. Note that we use *4* instead of *4BR* for the 4-bedroom condition because we don't know how that condition might appear in a listing. If some listings specify *4 BR* and we search for *4BR*, we would miss those listings. Of course, we will get some 5-bedroom, 4-bath homes as well with this query. Better to be a little more inclusive than too restrictive.

A Fact About Search Engines:

What we must remember about using search engines is that they index the content of *Web pages*, not the underlying *databases* that might be accessed from a page. Therefore, we would never limit our search to only those Web pages containing *all* of our required property specifications. If we took this approach, we would limit our universe to homes described only on one group's Web pages. We would not find database items that might be dynamically retrieved and presented on a Web page as a result of a query from within a site, such as from a FSBO or MLS site. First, we use search engines to find relevant sites, such as FSBO sites covering our location. Having exhausted those sources, we then can look to individual queries on the various search engines to find Web pages we might have missed otherwise. We make these searches as refined as possible without reducing our hit count to too few to be useful.

Wrapping It Up

At this point, because of your diligent study, you should know:

- The best FSBO sites and how to search them

- Where to find classified ads for FSBO properties

- How to use search engines a little more effectively to find the type of property you want

Now that you have learned how to search for a home to buy, it's time to move on. In Part II, "Let the Internet Help Sell Your Home," you will learn how to use the Internet to help sell your existing home, so that you'll have the money to buy that dream home you just found online.

PART II

Let the Internet Help Sell Your Home

CHAPTER 5

Sell Your Home Yourself and Save Thousands

You are an intelligent, capable, and computer-competent home-owner. You feel fully confident that you can sell your own home and save thousands in commission expense. In this chapter, let's see how to do it, using the Internet as a powerful marketing tool.

First, let's consider some of the issues involved in selling your home on your own as a For Sale By Owner, or a FSBO, as the industry refers to you.

What You'll Learn in This Chapter:

▶ The pros and cons of selling your own home

▶ How to price and market your home

▶ The best places to list your home on the Web

▶ Free online marketing resources you can use

So You Really Want to Be a FSBO

How to Say *FSBO*:

FSBO is the acronym of For Sale By Owner. It is universally pronounced *fizzbo* and is often used disparagingly by realtors. "Can you believe that after I showed them 10 houses, they went out and bought a [expletive deleted] fizzbo?"

A reality check is needed here to make sure that you understand what you're getting into by becoming a FSBO. What are the pros and cons of selling your own home? The most obvious advantage is saving the 6 or 7 percent in real estate commission. What about the other considerations? Table 5.1 summarizes the pros and cons.

Table 5.1   Pros and Cons of Selling as a FSBO

PRO	CON
Save commission expense of 6% to 7% (more or less)	Advertising and marketing expense is significant.
Control when property is shown	Possibly longer sell cycle than listing with realtor, with corresponding carrying costs (mortgage, utilities, maintenance, and so on).
Control how property is advertised	Inconvenience of showing on demand.
Negotiate directly with buyer	No access to MLS reduces access to buyers.
No listing contract with realtor	Negotiating directly with buyer may be difficult for you to do effectively.
	Difficult or impossible after relocating.
	Price is viewed by buyer as negotiable by commission amount saved.
	Price is assumed to be above market since it was not set by a realtor.

Saving 6 to 7 Percent: Is It Worth It?

Is it really worth all the disadvantages of selling your own home to save the real estate agent's commission? The answer depends on several common sense economic factors that you should understand.

- **Demand**   Consider the demand for your home. Is it in a desirable location with buyer interest, or is it a nice home in a remote or less desirable location? Are homes selling quickly in your neighborhood, or do they seem to stay on the market for months? Do agents solicit you to list your home? Ask for a listing presentation and see how an experienced realtor evaluates the prospects for a timely sale of your home.

- **Supply and Competition**   Are there many homes on the
  market in your area comparable to yours? What is the competition? Are you going to be competing with new construction
  in your immediate market? New homes in the same price
  range as yours can be tough competition because of builder
  concessions for closing costs and interest rate buydowns.
  Also, a new home near yours, offered at the same price as
  your used home, may make yours a second choice to a buyer
  (other factors such as size and features being equal). When
  competition is strong, listing with a real estate agent may be
  a better option. Agents can promote your home over the competing homes and sell your home's benefits against the flaws
  of the competing homes.

  Timing when to sell your home is important as well. If there
  are four homes in your immediate neighborhood for sale, you
  might consider waiting until two have sold before putting
  yours on the market. One interesting thing to consider is this:
  If there is a listed property for sale on or near your street,
  it can be an advantage for you, because buyers brought to the
  listed property by agents will see your For Sale By Owner
  sign.

- **Fair Market Pricing**   By far the biggest mistake a FSBO
  makes is overpricing the home. There are several reasons for
  this. Without access to the MLS to find comparable sales in
  the market area, most FSBOs don't have a realistic view of
  the prices homes similar to theirs are actually selling for.
  Recent sales of similar nearby properties is the most important factor in establishing market value. Furthermore, FSBOs
  tend to overvalue improvements made to the property.
  That $10,000 remodeling job to the master bedroom and bath
  you did two years ago does not add $10,000 of market price
  to your home. If neighboring homes are selling for $150,000
  with the same room count, livable square footage, and lot
  size, your home will not appraise for $10,000 more because
  of your remodeled master suite. The most valuable service a
  good listing agent provides, in addition to marketing, is to
  help you realistically price your home.

Remember:
Your savings will be
reduced by the cost
of your home being
on the market
longer than the
average for listed
properties.

Price It Yourself

Are there any ways you can get help in pricing without involving
a realtor? Let's check some online resources. There is a home sale
database service from INPHO, Inc., that a number of major portal
sites use to provide free home price data to Web surfers. Go to
Yahoo's Real Estate area and choose Home Values or go there
directly with this link:

http://realestate.yahoo.com/realestate/homevalues/

You can also go to an identical service provided by *The Wall
Street Journal* interactive edition with this direct link:

http://dowjones.homepricecheck.com/top.html

You will end up with the same search capability from INPHO at
either site. This service is also accessible from AOL, Excite, the
GO Network, and mortgage.com; don't bother checking all the
other sites; the data will be identical.

The initial search screen from Yahoo! conveniently shows which
states have coverage by the service. If your state is not listed, it is
probably a *non-disclosure* state, where real estate transactions do
not have prices disclosed in public records.

Any of the sites will give you a quick but limited look at prior
sale price data for a particular street. You can also search for prior
sales within a price range for a specified city or zip code. More
useful for our purpose of valuing a home to sell are two paid services and one additional free service, all of which are accessed
through iOwn, a mortgage site. This site has the important advantage of giving a free radius search for recent sales. When an
appraiser searches for comparable sales to help establish the market value of a home, he or she looks for recent sales (within the
last six months) in a .5 mile radius. If nearby sales are found and
the homes are reasonably similar, the appraiser must use these as
comparable sales in the assessment of your home's value.

By using iOwn's free search, you can get this same sales data. Go
to the search selection page directly at this URL:

http://rhs.iown.com/buy/rh_buy_index.htm

If this link has changed, start at *www.iown.com* and use the Shop for a Home and Check Recent Sale Prices menu selections to arrive at this page. From this page, select Address as the search type. You will get the search form shown in the following figure.

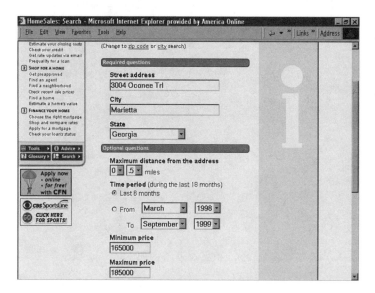

Use the iOwn search form to look for recent home sales within a .5 mile radius of your address.

For example, assume that your home is located at 3004 Oconee Trail in Marietta, Georgia. You paid $165,000 for it two years ago and now want to sell and trade up. You know from reading newspaper ads that homes like yours are selling in the mid $170s and you want to know about pricing your home for your market area. Submit the form as shown in the preceding figure; the result screen appears, listing several homes within a .5 mile radius with the date sold, the address, the selling price, and the distance away.

The Results table has a *Map* link at the top of the last column. If you go to the map, you can see the homes plotted on a map of the neighborhood, as shown in the following figure. A map similar to this one will be used by an appraiser as part of the formal appraisal. The map shows the proximity of the comparable properties used to establish the value of the home for the lender making the loan to the buyer of your home. Nearby, recent comps will always carry significant weight in the appraisal. In this example, we can see that right on the same street a home sold for

$173,500. Judging from the other nearby sales, it would appear that a price for your home in the mid-to-high $170s could be supported by the market.

Recent home sale data report from iOwn. Note the option to select the comparable properties for map display.

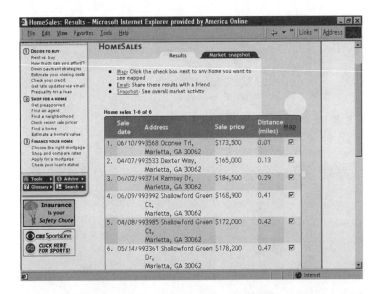

Use this map from iOwn to see where and for how much nearby homes have sold, so that you can price your home appropriately.

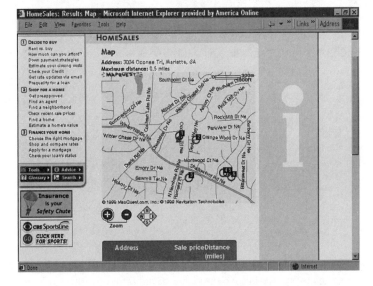

You can get a more refined valuation, similar to what an appraiser would do, by using iOwn's price estimation service. For $14.95, you can order a more detailed, appraisal-like report online by

going to Estimate a Home's Value on the search form or results
page. Check out the sample report and the methodology used.
This service has better coverage than others researched for this
book, and the price is reasonable.

You can also try *www.propertyview.com* to get a report with up to
30 sales of comparable homes in the past nine months, within a
half-mile radius of the target address. No sample report is available, but before you buy you get a count of the number of comparable sales found. This service is $9.95.

By using the free services and paying not more than $25, you can
get a good idea of how to price your home realistically for your
market. It would be well worth your time and money to do a thorough job of setting your price. Buyers who are interested in
homes in your area will have done their homework and will know
the prices of homes similar to yours. If your price is well above
the market, you will have a difficult time convincing a buyer
(if you have any) to pay your price. In addition, you run the risk
that the home will not appraise for your inflated price.

To be absolutely certain that your house is properly priced, you
can order a fee appraisal from a local appraiser. This report will
cost $250 to $350 or more but will give you a market value that
will assure purchasers at your price that they can get funded for a
mortgage. Because buyers are skeptical of owner's pricing anyway, it gives your price credibility and gives you negotiating
strength. (Why would you agree to sell below the appraised fair
market value of the property?) A fee appraisal could be the best
investment you make in marketing your home.

If you have determined that your home and location are in
demand, that the competition is not unbearable, and that you have
a fair market price in mind, you should definitely try selling your
home yourself. So let's cover what's involved in marketing your
home as a FSBO.

Prepare to Market, Show, and Sell

One of the benefits of using a top real estate agent to list and sell
your home is the marketing plan the agent will develop for your
home. Because you are not using an agent, you'll need to do your
own plan. At a minimum, it should address these items:

- Exterior improvements prior to going on the market

- Decorating or interior improvements needed

- Signage and flyers

- Using a lender to help your prospects buy

- Handling telephone inquiries

- Showing by appointment and open house showings

- Real estate agent policy

- Newspaper and other print advertising

- Online listings, advertising, and promotion

We will cover the last four items later in this chapter. Now, let's discuss the first five items of your plan.

Exterior and Interior Improvements

What you want to do and what the experts recommend is to make those improvements which (a) make your home competitive and (b) don't add expense you can't recover. Another goal is to eliminate maintenance or decorating issues that could become bargaining points in price negotiating.

Remember:

You are competing with every new home and listed property in your price range. Your home must have what agents call "curb appeal"—an appealing and inviting appearance seen from the street. And the interior of your home should appear immaculate to prospects.

You want your home, inside and out, to look every bit as appealing as the new model home your buyers will have seen in that new subdivision down the road. There is no need to remodel the master suite or put in all new bathroom fixtures—you won't get your investment back. However, you do need fresh paint inside and out and stunningly clean, neutral carpets or highly polished wood floors. (Do replace that circa-1970 gold shag carpet.) There should be absolutely no pet odors or stains.

Landscaping outside should be equal or superior to your neighbors and well groomed. Remember, you have only one property to sell. It should look as good as you can make it without unreasonable expense. Should you install an irrigation system for the lawn if you don't have one? No—you'll never recoup the expense.

Fix all minor exterior maintenance items like loose shingles, split or rotten decking, torn window screens, and so on. Should you Sheetrock and paint that unfinished garage? Absolutely; that is an inexpensive and easy improvement that upgrades your home. (Go look at some new model homes in your price range to see the competition's curb appeal and interior quality.)

There are two good sources of information online about how to prepare your home for sale. Ed Osgood, who is a former real estate broker and who bills himself as the "Real Estate Rebel," publishes a hard-hitting, nuts-and-bolts guide to selling your own home. Ed offers very sound advice for FSBO sellers. You can find his $24.95, downloadable report, "Real Estate Secrets," at this URL:

> *www.fsbotips.com*

You can preview some of his material at this site, under the heading Real Estate Secrets:

> *www.homeportfoliojunction.com*

This second site is an excellent FSBO listing site that we will be discussing later.

Another good source of seller information comes from *www.homegain.com*, which has a Sellers Library with free articles you can read or print. Robert Bruss, the syndicated newspaper real estate columnist, contributes articles to this site. He also has a site with many useful articles for home sellers at very nominal cost.

You can go to his site directly at *https://secure.inman.com/bruss* or link to his site from the HomeGain.com Home Seller Library page.

One of the best online sources of free information for selling your home is found on Owners.com in their online Sellers Handbook. We will be covering this site, which is the premier FSBO listing site on the Internet, in detail later in this chapter.

Signage and Flyers

Real estate agents know that the yard sign alone accounts for 60 to 70 percent of sales. Some listing agents have no more of a marketing plan than a sign in your yard and your listing in the MLS.

Use These Freebies:

Be sure to use the free information available to home sellers from HomeGain.com's Home Seller Library and from Owners.com's Sellers Handbook. Print the articles and file them in your home marketing notebook for permanent reference.

Did You See That Sign?

There is a better than 60 percent probability that your home will sell directly from your yard sign. Make the sign big and use more than one sign, including directional signs from major roads. Buyers find For Sale By Owner directional signs hard to resist as they drive through neighborhoods of interest.

Your sign is important and should be big, bold, and prominent. Directional signs are necessary to direct traffic to your home. You can have more than one yard sign, and you can be different by putting your asking price on the sign or the estimated monthly payment required. A little later, we'll discuss working with a lender to help you with offering appropriate financing and to screen and prequalify your prospects.

In addition to your sign or signs, you must develop and attach flyers to your sign. Waterproof tubes and containers are available at office supply stores. Attach this "take one" container to your sign and fill it with flyers. Include a photo, complete descriptive information, and telephone numbers on your flyers.

Buyers crave information, so satisfy this need with a first-rate flyer. Their memories will be hazy, and your home may get confused with others they visit or drive past. Make your flyer a portable, positive memory of your home. Include every possible feature and emotional benefit of your property in your flyer. It should be much more than a listing fact sheet—it should be as powerful a sales brochure as you can make it.

Getting Help from Lenders

One of your most effective marketing partners can be a competent loan officer from a full-service mortgage lender. By *full-service* I mean either a mortgage broker or a mortgage banker who offers all possible loan programs, including FHA, VA, conforming, non-conforming, and subprime. (These terms, if unfamiliar to you, are explained in Chapter 7, "Financing Your Dream Home.")

Get Free Professional Help:

Unless there is a refinance boom going on, you can get a competent mortgage loan officer to help you market your home. These professionals can really help you, so take advantage of their free advice and services.

A good loan officer can develop financing alternatives for your home, can screen and prequalify prospects for you, can make flyers for you, will attend your open house, and do it all for free. Your prospects will understand what is required to buy your home—and if you let the loan officer screen your prospects, you won't waste your time with unqualified, hopeless buyers. You benefit from the lender's expertise and he gets a stream of loan prospects. It's a win-win relationship.

Handling Telephone Inquiries

There are two ways to deal with the telephone inquiry. You can provide numbers where you can be reached days and evenings and field the calls in person. Or you can have a recorded message. What direct marketing experts recommend, no matter what you are selling with an advertised telephone number, is to have an informational recording after which the caller leaves a recorded message. This info line is usually advertised as a 24-hour recorded message or free recorded information. You can use this strategy with your FSBO sign and classified advertising.

Using a recorded message increases response because callers know they don't have to talk to a salesperson (you, in this case), and they can remain anonymous if they so choose. As Ed Osgood points out in "Real Estate Secrets," this recording gives you the chance to pitch the emotional features and benefits of your home, without interruption, in a three- or four-minute presentation to the caller. You are in control and can screen respondents further by saying that you will take appointments only from qualified buyers. By using a recorded message, you will be able to call prospects back at a time convenient to you and will not miss any calls from serious prospects.

Showing by Appointment and Open House Showings

Schedule back-to-back appointments, if possible, to generate a sense of urgency and demand for your home. Buyers do not want to miss out on a good deal, and you want each prospect to know, by observation, that you have more than one person interested. Once a prospect arrives for an appointment, any real estate agent will tell you that you should not follow buyers around as they look at your home. Better yet, you should not even be present at a showing. You can introduce yourself, point out some less-obvious benefits, and then invite the buyers to look around on their own. You can answer questions after they have looked and talked privately. The longer they stay, the more interested they are—do not hover around them.

Holding an open house is a good way to show your home to multiple prospects who have called. You can get them all to arrive during a one- or two-hour period on a Saturday or Sunday after-

Telephone Tip:

Answer live or call back immediately if you are not using an info line recorded message. Always respond as soon as possible so that you get to your prospects while they're "hot." Prospects cool off quickly, as every realtor knows.

Remember:

Give your prospects privacy as they look at your home. Don't follow them around. The longer they stay, the more they are interested.

A Bird in Hand:

A quick sale to an agent's buyer at full price may well be worth the commission you'll pay. Remember that you have both carrying costs and opportunity costs of keeping your home on the market.

noon. Simply advertising an open house will probably draw more curious neighbors and lookie-loos than serious prospects.

Being CO-OPerative

One issue you must deal with is the real estate agent issue. What will you do if an agent requests a showing for a prospective buyer? The agent will want you to sign a one-time showing or listing agreement to guarantee his or her commission if the buyer makes an offer, now or later on. You should welcome agents' buyers and agree to pay some amount of commission; the closer to the normal split an agent will get, the more likely it is that the agent will actually try to sell your home.

When an agent sells another company's listing, it is called a co-op (short for *co-operative*) sale. Agents split the commission 50/50.

Think of it from the agent's perspective. Why should she let her buyers see and buy your home for less than she could get by selling a listed property on a co-op? Unless the agent does not have a buyer's agreement and is afraid of losing the prospect to you, she is not likely to cut her potential commission to sell your home to her buyers. This is a personal matter for you to decide. Can you afford to pay 3 or 3.5 percent for a quick sale to a qualified buyer? You should seriously consider the carrying cost of keeping your property on the market if you are not getting traffic and agents have interested buyers.

Listing Your Home on the Internet

Reminder:

By itself, a FSBO listing is not very likely to quickly produce a buyer for your home. It should be *one* of your marketing tools but not the only one.

You will want to list your home on some of the listing sites discussed in this section. I want to emphasize that an online listing is one and only one of your marketing tools. It is the combination of signage, advertising, online listings, and promotion that will sell your home. With that understood, let's find the best places to list your home.

If you wanted to sell your baseball card collection or that family heirloom Hummel figurine, where would you go on the Internet? To eBay, of course. Why? Because eBay has the most sellers and buyers on its auction site, by far, of any place on the Web. eBay *is* the auction market. Every other auction site is miniscule by comparison. Is there any place on the Internet that would qualify as the eBay of FSBO real estate? The answer is *yes* and the site is at *www.owners.com*. We've been to this site before, in Chapter 4, "How to Find the Perfect FSBO Property," when we were searching for a FSBO home.

The opening page of the Owners.com FSBO site. This site is destined to become the premier nationwide MLS for FSBOs.

Owners.com (formerly Abele Owners' Network) claims to have marketed over 250,000 homes since 1996. By my estimate, they have about 27,000 active listings, far and away the most of any FSBO site on the Net. They recently (September 1999) partnered with AOL to become the source for Private Homes for Sale in AOL's ClassifiedsPlus category. With exposure to 20 million AOL subscribers, Owners.com is well positioned to become the first true national FSBO listing site.

Owners.com is already the dominant FSBO site, with more listings and more services than any other FSBO site. It is dwarfed by Realtor.com with 1.3 million real estate agent listings, but only about 15 to 20 percent of home sellers attempt to sell as FSBOs. The total market for FSBO listings is about 900,000, so Owners.com already has a 3 percent market share. This site will grow based on the "if you build it, they will come" networking model, just as eBay did.

What does Owners.com offer you as a FSBO? Table 5.2 summarizes your options.

Table 5.2   Listing Options Offered by Owners.com

Service Option	Cost
LIMITED	**Free**
One (1) picture, Lowest priority in search results, free distribution on Yahoo!	
3-month listing	
STANDARD	**$89**
One (1) picture, Priority in search results, customized yard sign with stake, free distribution on Yahoo!	
3-month listing, renewable	
PREMIER	**$139**
Five (5) pictures, Priority in search results, free distribution on Yahoo!, customized yard sign with stake, open house kit including open house rider and directional signs (2), flyer holder attached to sign, *For Sale by Owner Kit* book by Robert Irwin	
3-month listing, renewable	

You may be able to find a lower-cost listing package somewhere else, but you won't get the exposure you get with Owners.com. This is *the place* for your paid listing. (Remember those 20 million AOL users?) The help and information you get at this site set it apart from the competition as well. At the very least, you must use their free listing service. When you select the List My Home button on the Owners.com opening page, you are taken to the listing options page, shown in the next figure.

Why not take a break from reading now and go list your home online and see how easy it is?

Try It Yourself ▼

1. From the Owners.com listing options page, select How to List Your Home from the right side of the window, under the List Your Home! heading.

2. Follow the instructions given on the pages that follow to register and enter your listing information.

   You will be given an opportunity to email your digital images (or send photos by postal mail, to be scanned for you at Owners.com for no extra charge).

3. You can submit some limited HTML in your description, so you may want to plan your description and its formatting before you reach the listing input screen. The whole procedure is easy to follow, and you get to preview and correct your listing before submitting it.

This online listing should not take more than 10 to 15 minutes at the most for you to complete.

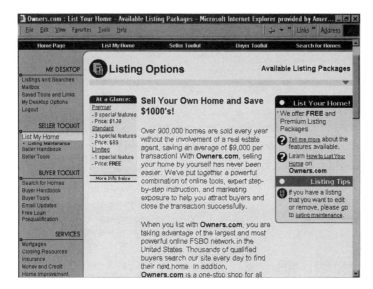

This is the listing options page from Owners.com—the starting point for entering your listing.

Now let's look at getting maximum passive exposure by listing at the best free and paid FSBO sites.

Free Listing Sites

Obviously, time permitting, we want to list on as many free sites as possible. Table 5.3 shows you where to go. The sites with free picture(s) options should be your first priority. You should list at every possible site that accommodates your requirements.

Table 5.3   Free FSBO Listing Sites

Site URL	Features
www.owners.com	1 picture, 3-month listing
www.freehomelistings.com	No picture, list until sold, add 1 picture for $9.95/mo, 2 pictures for $14.95/mo

continues

Table 5.3   Continued

Site URL	Features
www.homeportfoliojunction.com (Advanced Real Estate Listing Service)	1 picture, list until sold, many upgrades, paid packages and services, including Web page
www.fsboworldnet.com	1 picture, list until sold, donation of $10 or more to homeless organization requested
www.comprealty.com	No picture, 6-month listing, upgrade to 1 photo for $39, 2 to 5 photos for $59
www.advertise-free.com	No picture, 90-day listing, upgrade to 1 photo for $5, 2 photos for $8, 3 photos for $10
www.dotcomusa.com	No picture, 30-day listing, free email notice when listing is viewed
www.forsalebyownernetwork.com	1 picture, list until sold
www.homesaledirect.com	30 days free, 1 photo scanned for you or up to 6 photos uploaded by you, link for your Web site, upgrade $19.95 for list until sold
www.theadnet.com	No picture, free classified ad-type listing, deleted after 30 days
www.efsbo.com	60-day free classified listing, no picture, upgrades available

There is no compelling reason not to use *all* these free listing sites for your own listing. It will take some effort to get your listing submitted to each site in the format required by each, but you should seriously consider using every free advertising opportunity.

Paid Listing Sites

Tip:

My advice is to avoid monthly listing charges and pay a one-time fee for a "list until sold" package with the FSBO sites.

In addition to Owners.com (a must-do site because of its popularity), where should you pay for an online FSBO listing? Here are the recommended top sites, with cost and features shown. Note that some are duplicates of the free sites, which give you a basic free listing but offer to sell added features and services.

Remember that the likelihood of selling your home directly as a result of a buyer searching one of these sites is relatively low, so evaluate carefully and select one or two more sites to use. You will also want to consider using a local FSBO site that specializes in your community or state. Go to *www.fsboguide.com* and select your state to see if a local FSBO site is available that specializes in your area.

The best paid FSBO sites to consider (in addition to Owners.com) are listed in Table 5.4.

Table 5.4   Paid FSBO Listing Sites

URL	Cost
www.efsbo.com	**$39 package:** 90-day listing with 2 pictures for $39
	$59 package: 90-day listing, 5 photos, 1 yard sign, private URL (for example, *http://www.eFSBO.com/myhouse*)
	$79 package: 120-day listing, 10 photos, 1 yard sign, private URL
	$199 package: 180-day listing, 15 photos, 2 yard signs, free photo development and scanning, private URL
www.by-owner-ol.com	**$99 package:** list until sold, 5 photos, yard sign, directional sign, take-one tube, hit counter
	$50 package: as above but no signs
	$25 package: 1 photo, 6-month listing
www.buyowner.com	**$79 package:** 8 pictures, list until sold (prices may differ in some franchised areas)
www.homeportfoliojunction.com	**$65 package:** 6 pictures, list until sold, free scanning, up to 4 additional photos at $5 each, unlimited text, email and Web page links, private URL, hit counter
	$95 package: 12-photo virtual tour presentation, plus the above

When considering these paid listing sites, if you do not have your own Web page to promote your property, then one of the sites that offer a private URL or link to the page will be beneficial. You can reference this private URL in your other advertising and promotional efforts.

You are going to have to become an online marketer to promote your home, which is our next topic.

FSBO Package Deal:

For a good deal on a combination picture listing, sign, and seller information, check out FSBO.com's package. This up-and-coming site has only a couple thousand listings nationwide, but their offer is compelling: For $19.95, you get a full listing with one picture that remains online until the property is sold; you also get a hot link to your Web site. Add a yard sign for another $19.95, or get the $49.95 bundle, which includes the listing, the sign, a change request, and two seller's guides. Go to *www.fsbo.com* now to see for yourself.

Become an Online Marketer

You need to take advantage of the active and passive marketing tools available online. One of the benefits of the growth of the Internet and the ease of access to the WWW is that a Web page can become an online color brochure for whatever you are selling. Whether you develop your own Web page for your listing or use a private URL from one of the FSBO services, your prospects have immediate access to complete information about your property for sale.

The goal of all your promotion and advertising efforts, online and offline, is to get your prospects to view your property online and then contact you for a showing appointment.

A Picture Really Is Worth a Thousand Words

The More Pictures, the Better:

The Web is a visual place. Give your buyer prospects plenty to look at. Surfers find additional photos hard to resist while browsing.

No home has ever been sold by the written description alone. Homes must be *seen* to be sold. The first step to generating enough interest for your prospects to make an appointment is to properly present your home with pictures. The WWW is a graphic medium. Quality, high-resolution photography is needed. Don't waste your advertising and promotional money and effort on text-only presentations. In real estate, a picture really *is* worth a thousand words.

Virtual Tours Are Even Better

One or two static pictures of your home on a listing site or your own home page is definitely better than a text-only description. A virtual tour is even better and gives the prospect a sense of having seen or walked through your home.

Virtual tours can be created from a series of exterior and interior photos, sequentially displayed in one window or in a photo album– or catalog-style layout. A more dramatic technology is panoramic photography, which provides a 360-degree seamless photograph that can be zoomed and panned by the viewer. This technology is still new and requires special digital camera equipment and software to implement. We discussed the two major vendors of this technology, bamboo.com and IPIX, in "Take a Virtual Tour," in Chapter 3, "For Buyers: How to Find Your Dream Home." IPIX is the vendor for FSBOs who want to add virtual tours to their Web sites; bamboo.com sells only to realtors.

For $95, IPIX will have a contract photographer take the panoramic digital photography for your home. Then you can add the virtual tour capability to your own Web site. Alternatively, if you have the compatible digital camera equipment, you can buy the IPIX software ($200) for creating the panoramic views from your own photography. To get an idea of the power of this technology for viewing a home, go to *www.vrrealty.com* and see how they are using virtual tours to market upscale homes in San Francisco. The opening page of this site is shown in the next figure and is definitely worth a visit to see the application of virtual tour technology.

For another approach to virtual tours, using static images, go to *www.homeportfoliojunction.com* and select Virtual Property Tours to see an example of that company's version of a virtual tour.

Advertising and Promoting Your Listing

At the risk of being redundant, I'll repeat the caveat that listing your home on one or more FSBO listing sites is only one—albeit a potent one—of your marketing tools. By itself, online listing of your home is not as effective at generating offers as it will be when you combine that technique with other advertising and promotions.

Your FSBO listing is online information about your property, accessible by anyone with Internet access. You need to direct prospects to your listing and to your Web site, if you have one.

The www.vrrealty. com *site is where IPIX virtual tours are used to market San Francisco homes.*

At a minimum, your advertising must consist of a series of Sunday classified ads and flyers attached to your sign. If you will work with agents, then you should fax flyers to real estate offices serving your location.

Your classified newspaper advertising, your yard sign, and your flyer should direct prospects to your online listing or Web site. A typical classified ad for your property could take this form:

> *[Area or address] [$Price]* **For Sale by Owner.***[Brief description here]* **Call 123-555-1212 for 24hr recorded message. See online at** *[Web site or FSBO site's private URL for your listing here] or* **See listing #12345 at** *[FSBO site home page URL].* **No agents please.** *[Or* **Agents welcome.***] [Other phone numbers]*

Note that you are screening prospects immediately by location and price, you give them an opportunity to hear your recorded sales presentation, and then you direct them to your online presentation. Every ad or flyer should contain these same elements.

Your sign should have your FSBO listing site and listing ID# shown, as well as the URL of your own Web site used to promote the property. This brings us to the question of whether or not you should have a Web site to promote your property.

Your Own Web Site: Do You Need One?

If you have the patience and the technical skill to create a Web site to promote your property, by all means do so. Most Internet service providers (and AOL) offer personal Web pages for free. AOL has free software (Hotdog Express) that you can download for creating your own Web site. If your ISP does not offer a free Web page service and software support for creating it, there are many other free Web page hosting services on the Internet.

Here are some of the free hosting sites you can check out. Each offers site creation software or dynamic Web page creation and other Web page design aids:

- *www.spree.com*

- *www.homestead.com*

- *www.tripod.com*

- *www.webjump.com*

- *http://geocities.yahoo.com/home*

- *www.angelfire.com*

- *www.hotbot.com*

Because you can get a free Web page, free software, or online site creation, there is really nothing to keep you from developing your own promotional page for your home for sale. Nothing, that is, except the time and effort needed to create your site. I'll bet you can create your own page, complete with photos (if you have a scanner), in less than one hour. The promotional benefits of having your own home page are truly worth this investment of time and effort.

Classified Ads

As mentioned earlier, a classified ad in the Sunday real estate section of your local newspaper is your primary *print* advertising medium. You should plan on running for four to eight weeks consecutively, varying the ad slightly from week to week.
This will be your major expense in marketing your home. Check with your local paper about packaged rates and volume discounts.

Do not waste your money on *space ads* (also known as *display ads*) in your newspaper. A properly written classified ad will work just as well as the more expensive space ad.

Using Email and Fax Broadcast

You will definitely need to have your email address in your online FSBO listing. You may want to use email contact only for privacy reasons (instead of using your telephone numbers in your listing). You may also want to use one of the free email services if your only email address is on your company's server. Again, this is a privacy issue. You might want to direct all buyer prospects to another email address. There are plenty of free email sites. A directory of hundreds of free email sites is found at this URL:

www.emailaddresses.com

If you are willing to work with real estate agents, you should email your flyer or listing information to individual agents who advertise their email addresses and to real estate offices. In addition, you should fax your flyer to real estate offices in your market area. If you have fax software such as WinFax Pro, you can set up a fax broadcast of your flyer to real estate agents and offices. Once it is set up, you can fax to the offices weekly, because different agents will probably see the flyer each time you broadcast.

Free Virtual Fax Numbers Available:

While we are discussing faxes, if you don't have fax software and the ability to *receive* (not send) faxes on your computer and want to have that capability, get a free universal fax number from this site:

www.messageclick.com

You will be able to receive faxes through email as well as receive voice mail. If you don't have a fax machine at home, you never know when a "virtual fax" like this one might be helpful.

Wrapping It Up

In this chapter, you learned about selling your home as a FSBO, what free and paid online listing services to use, and other techniques to market your property online.

If you made it this far, you are ready to become a FSBO. However, if timing, relocation issues, or the fact that you just can't be bothered selling your own home is an issue, you will need the services of a real estate agent. How to find an agent and help him or her sell your home are the main topics of Chapter 6, "Helping Your Realtor Sell Your Home." If you are not going to list with an agent, you can skip the next chapter.

CHAPTER 6

Helping Your Realtor Sell Your Home

Do You Need to List with an Agent?

There may be some compelling reasons for you to use an agent to sell your home rather than attempting to sell it yourself (or to continue to try on your own). You may have a severe time constraint; if you failed as a FSBO and must sell, listing is your next logical choice. (Auctioning the property is also a choice, but not one that will likely net you more than an agent-assisted sale.) Most FSBOs who end up listing with an agent do so because of time constraints.

Another possibility is that you may have already relocated and physically can't function as a FSBO. Other reasons to list your property are if it is a slow market or if your property is a difficult sell and you need the exposure in the MLS to have a better chance of reaching buyers. Let's look at the listing issue more closely.

Pros and Cons of Listing

In looking at the pros and cons of listing, the big con is the 6 or 7 percent commission you are going to pay. Another negative is having a listing contract that ties you to an agent for up to 180 days. This can be a problem if the agent is not marketing your home effectively and you have no way out of the listing contract. There is nothing more frustrating than having failed to sell your home yourself, then to list with an agent and have no offers for three or four months. So, the length of the listing contract and the commission are the big negatives; you should negotiate accordingly to try to reduce both, if you possibly can.

On the positive side of the ledger, there are some major benefits of listing with an agent:

- Your home will be listed on the MLS (multiple listing service) and available for every agent to find.

- A good agent will advertise your home and promote it to other agents within his company and to other brokers.

- Your agent (and other agents) will show your home without your involvement and actively attempt to sell your home, since he is not paid unless the home sells.

- Your agent will negotiate on your behalf with the buyer's agent and attempt to get the highest price for your home.

- The agent will handle the various details of closing the sale, including arranging the closing and ordering or helping you with required inspections, disclosures, water and septic tests (if required), and other details.

- If you have already moved, the agent can arrange for the sale under limited power of attorney so that you do not have to travel back to the closing.

As it stands today, fewer than 20 percent of home sales are made by owners selling their own homes. This will change as the Internet continues to erode the advantage agents have with the MLS. This book's intent is to help you be successful as a FSBO if you choose to sell your own home. However, for some of the reasons discussed, you may need the services of a real estate agent. If you do use an agent, you can use the Internet to help find a good real estate agent. (Some cynics might call the term *good real estate agent* an oxymoron, but we won't get into that debate here.)

Use the Net to Find a Good Listing Agent

Obviously you can solicit local real estate offices and use referrals from friends and business associates to find a listing agent for your home. You also can use the Internet to anonymously evaluate proposals from agents. This approach has some advantages; you can choose whom to contact after screening proposals, rather than starting with personal interviews. Real estate agents are some of the most persistent and aggressive salespeople you will ever deal with. If several local agents know you want to list your home, they will bombard you with phone calls, proposals, and refrigerator magnets. We can use an innovative online service called HomeGain.com to search for agents. Point your browser to *www.homegain.com* to reach the company's home page. Notice in the following figure what services they offer to home sellers.

A Seller's Resource:

HomeGain.com is an information site dedicated to home sellers. Besides its agent evaluation service, there are other worthwhile tools for sellers here. Read a few of the articles in the Sellers Library to pick up some good advice.

HomeGain.com offers various selling tools, including an agent evaluation service.

Of greatest interest to us is the Agent Evaluator service. To use this service, you register with HomeGain.com and enter an information profile about your property and your requirements. Your identity is kept confidential. Agents respond to your profile with proposals that you can screen online. The next figure shows the steps in this process.

HomeGain.com was started in April 1999; it should grow in popularity and functionality as it is discovered and as the agent enrollment grows. Agents and brokers in your area may not know about HomeGain.com or may choose not to participate

Try Contacting Agents by Email Only:

You can try the anonymous listing proposal technique by using email. Find some prominent agents' email addresses from your local Board of Realtors Web site or from newspaper ads. Email these agents a request for a listing proposal using the HomeGain.com profile model. Insist on an email response first and then see if you are interested in further contact with the agent. Don't include your telephone number.

in the service. You may want to suggest anonymously to several local brokers that you will be listing your $850,000 home soon and want to evaluate agent proposals using the HomeGain.com service. Ask agents if they are currently members of HomeGain.com. If none are, they will be soon—if only to get a chance to list your home.

Steps for using HomeGain.com for agent evaluation. The system keeps you in control of the process without being pressured by the agents you evaluate.

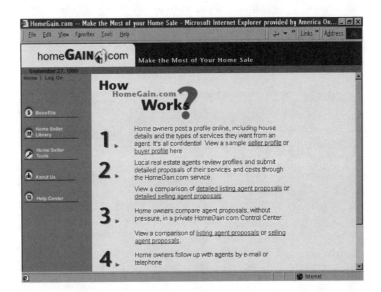

Get Listing Presentations

After you have selected, by whatever means, a short list of three or four agents to interview, ask for a listing presentation, including a Comparative Market Analysis (CMA) and a marketing plan for your property. Make these agents work to get your business— after all, they stand to make a minimum of 3 to 3.5 percent of your selling price as commission if they get the listing. If they sell your listing, they get the full 6 or 7 percent commission. You should expect a thoroughly professional and comprehensive presentation.

You will need to evaluate the various proposals based on the CMA, the marketing plan, and the agent's qualifications and reputation. You should also check to make certain that the agent's license is in good standing with the state real estate commission.

For quick access online to 47 of the 50 state licensing authorities, go to the Association of Real Estate Licensing Law Officials at *www.arello.org* and select Directory. You'll find addresses, telephone numbers, and links to Web sites for each state licensing entity.

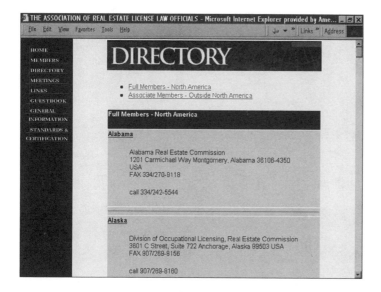

Use the directory at www.arello.org to find the real estate licensing authority in your state.

The Comparative Market Analysis

Because pricing your home properly is critical to selling it successfully, your agent should do a competent job of establishing your home's price through a comparison of recent sales of comparable homes. This analysis is known in the industry by the standard term Comparative Market Analysis (CMA).

A good agent will have software available to help generate a CMA with at least three price-adjusted, comparable, sold properties. The report should show these properties in a side-by-side, spreadsheet-like format.

Do Your Homework:

In Chapter 5, "Sell Your Home Yourself and Save Thousands," we learned ways to research comparables online and get free and low cost valuations. You should still do this research on your own to have a benchmark for assessing the accuracy of the agents' CMA proposals.

A sample CMA report compares your property with several comparable properties sold in your area.

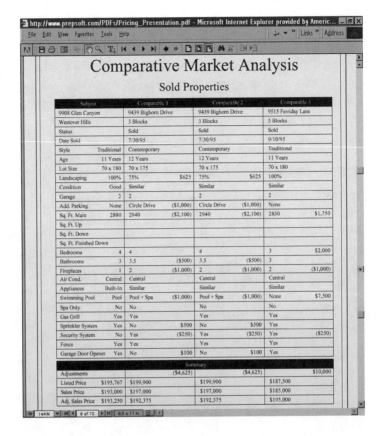

When comparable properties are used in an appraisal, they are adjusted in price by features to make them comparable to the subject property. A good CMA will approximate what an actual appraiser would do in appraising the property. Here's how adjustments are made:

- When a comparable property has a feature that the subject property does not have, an estimated value is *subtracted* from the comparable's selling price. Note the $1,000 negative adjustment for the extra fireplace each comparable has in the sample CMA shown.

- When the subject property has a feature that the comparable property does not have, a value is *added* to the comparable's price. Note that Comparable #3 has a $2,000 addition because it has only 3 bedrooms instead of 4.

- A net positive or negative adjustment is added to or subtracted from the selling prices of the comparables to arrive at adjusted prices for the comparables. Note that negative adjustments are shown in parentheses, such as (1,000) for a negative $1,000 adjustment.

- The adjusted comparable prices are averaged to get an estimated selling price for the subject property (see the summary section at the bottom of the example).

Be aware that unadjusted comparables are not really comparable properties in terms of market value. Let's say that your neighbor's 3-bedroom, 2-bath home sold for $150,000 and that he had a 2-car garage and a finished basement. Your home is about the same size, with 3 bedrooms and 2 baths, but has no garage or basement. Your home will not command the same market price.

Doing your own research and having a realistic price in mind are important for evaluating the CMA, because you must be wary of too-low or too-high evaluations. Consider these issues:

Caution:

If your prospective agent does not understand what adjusted comparable properties are, get another agent.

- Any idiot can sell a house priced 10 to 15 percent below fair market value. If an agent is desperate for a quick sale, you might get a low estimate, particularly if the agent does not know you are comparison shopping for an agent. Watch out for this situation.

- You think your home's fair market value is $150,000, and an agent's CMA estimate is for a sale price of $165,000—10 percent higher than your expectation. This may be a pleasant surprise to you, but if you have done your homework, you should be suspicious. The agent may be incompetent at developing an accurate CMA or may be trying to "buy the listing." This is a trick agents use when they know you are comparing agent proposals. By promising to get you a higher price for your home, they hope to win the competition to get your listing.

You can challenge the higher-than-normal price simply by saying to the agent, "I didn't think my home was worth this much. Can you really sell it at that price within 30 to 60 days without reducing the price?" If the agent assures you that she can, claiming to have buyer interest now in your neighborhood or whatever, then say, "That's great, but I'm skeptical. What do you say we list it on a 30-day trial listing contract and see how many showings and offers we get at that price?" Watch how the agent squirms and backpedals and starts insisting on a 120- or 180-day listing because of advertising schedules, company policy, and so on.

Your challenge will reveal the agent's real strategy of overpricing to get the listing for 180 days and then, after 60 days of no offers, suggesting a price cut to stimulate interest in the property.

Don't be seduced by the overly optimistic sales price an agent claims to be able to get for you. Defeat the strategy by insisting on a short, 30- to 60-day trial listing contract. If the agent says that's not possible, say "Can't we agree to renew the listing after 60 days?" Remember that you will be handing the listing agent a contract worth thousands of dollars. *Don't be shy about playing hard ball with real estate agents.*

The Marketing Plan: More than a Sign?

Your agent's listing presentation should include a plan of how your home will be marketed. Installing a yard sign with the agent's picture on it and inserting your listing into MLS is not a marketing plan. You should insist on an actual plan with definite advertising schedules and media defined in writing.

You will be able to tell from the agent's plan (if there is one) if you are dealing with a seasoned professional or a neophyte. Ask the agent what changes will be made to the marketing plan if you sign a 120- or 180-day listing and there are no offers in the first 30 to 60 days. Will a price reduction be required, or will the agent increase the advertising frequency and number of media?

The plan should include, at a minimum, the following elements:

- Online advertising at Realtor.com

- An open house schedule

- Real estate rack magazine advertising

- Newspaper classified and space advertising

- Promotion to other local real estate offices

The Truth About Open Houses:

Your agent says she'll hold an open house for your home for the next four consecutive Sundays after you list with her. Should you be impressed with this aggressive marketing? Yes and no. On the positive side, the agent thinks enough of your home to attract buyer traffic with open house signs. Sadly, however, this aggressive marketing is more for the agent's benefit than yours. Very few homes are sold to open house visitors, but agents pick up buyer and seller prospects at these events. If your home is a prime property and priced to sell, you *may* get offers from open house prospects. The reality is that, more often than not, you are giving your agent a lovely environment for recruiting prospects, while you are banished from your own home on a Sunday afternoon.

If there is no defined advertising and promotion plan *in writing*, then there is no plan, no matter what the agent tells you he will do. Don't work with an agent who has only a yard sign plan for selling your home.

The Agent's and Broker's Reputations

The next criteria to evaluate in selecting a listing agent are the agent's and the broker's reputations. When checking the agent's license with the state authority, ask if the broker for whom the agent works is in good standing. You may also be able to inquire at the local board of realtors about complaints or disciplinary actions against the agent and broker in question.

There are no absolute assurances about reputation. Recent sellers who have used the listing agent and broker are your best sources of information. But if you ask the agent for the names of other sellers she has helped, you won't hear about the unsuccessful listings that stayed on the market 18 months or never sold. If the agent is prominent in your market area, and if you have seen some of her signs, drive around some Saturday afternoon and ask a homeowner or two how they assess the agent's performance.

The length of time in the business and number of homes sold in the past year are valid questions to ask your agent. How many current listings the agent has is another good question, as is average time on the market. Ask the agent if he is willing to give you a printout from the MLS of each of his listings sold in the past 12 months and of those currently on the market. Only a top professional with nothing to hide will do this for you. From these listing printouts, you can determine the days on the market for each sold and current listing.

The Listing Agreement

When you engage the services of a real estate agent to sell your home, you enter into a binding contract known as a *listing agreement*. The agreement is not just a formality, as your smiling agent may suggest—it is a contract with specific and binding terms that can bedevil you for six months or more if you are not careful. This agreement defines the agent's commission and your obligations. You must understand the terms and conditions and realize that, no matter what the agent represents to you verbally, the written listing agreement will prevail.

After you have decided to use the agent, you should use this tactic before signing the listing agreement: Tell the agent that your personal attorney has advised you never to sign any contractual agreement without his review. You are going to need to take the listing agreement to your attorney before you can sign it, and this will take a day or two. If the agent will not leave a copy of the agreement with you, insisting that she must get a signature now, well, you know what to do: Show her the door.

Remember:

A co-op sale is when another agent sells your agent's listing of your home. The commission you pay is split 50/50 between the listing agent and the selling agent. You don't care who gets the commission as long as you get your price. Beware of a listing agent who denigrates a co-op offer. Remember, the listing agent gets only half the commission on a co-op. If she sells her own listing, she gets it all.

Your Agent's Accounts Receivable

The listing contract is just like an account receivable for the listing agent. If you sign a 120- or 180-day listing agreement and the home is priced realistically, the agent knows with some certainty that he can do nothing and get at least a co-op sale before the listing expires. Agents want the longest possible listing contract because it's like money in the bank. You, on the other hand, want the shortest possible agreement, because pulling the listing away is the only leverage you have to make the agent work hard and fast to sell your home. Every day your home sits on the market costs you money. *Get the shortest possible listing agreement you can negotiate.*

Everything Is Negotiable

Everything in a listing agreement, including the agent's commission, is negotiable. Don't fall for the ploy that "the company requires us to list for 180 days and charge 7 percent commission." If you make a concession, such as listing for longer than 60 days, get a concession in return, such as a lower commission or more advertising. Make the agent understand that you are interviewing several agents and that all have been willing to negotiate. If the agent wants your business, he will have to negotiate, just like the other agents. We are talking about the biggest personal financial transaction you will ever make, so don't be intimidated.

Remember that the agent stands to make thousands of dollars in commission from the sale of your home. Negotiate *everything* and play hard ball. If you offend an agent with your tough negotiating, don't worry about it. There are hundreds more to choose from.

Avoid Exclusives

An agent might attempt to get you to sign an exclusive listing, which precludes co-op sales by other agents. This is highly unlikely, but watch out for it in smaller markets, where a broker may not belong to an MLS or where there is no MLS.

If you have been acting as a FSBO and have some prospects, avoid the agent's "exclusive right to sell" language for these prospects. You will have to list specifically the names of buyers who are excluded from the terms of the listing agreement. If that prospect you almost sold to when you were a FSBO comes back, you want to be able to sell to him without paying a commission.

How to Make a Lazy Agent Work Harder

The only way to make a lazy listing agent work harder is to threaten not to renew the listing when it expires. If you have negotiated a 60- to 90-day or shorter agreement and you have had no showings—or less than one per week in the first 30 days—tell the agent you are not going to renew if you don't get an offer in the next 30 days. If she can't sell your home in 60 days (especially if the average time on the market is 30 to 60 days), you need a new agent.

Promote Your Realtor's Listing Online

You have chosen an agent and signed a 60- or 90-day listing agreement. It's been three weeks and nothing is happening. Maybe you had a few showings but no offers. This is a typical pattern. Your objective is to sell your house at full price as quickly as possible. Why not help your agent from day one? It is in your interest to do so.

You Are a Better Online Marketer

I can assure you that you are a better online marketer of your property than your agent is, especially after your diligence in reading and working through this book. Put this knowledge to work by helping your agent with online marketing of the property.

Advertise and Promote Your Listing

Use the free listing sites covered in Chapter 5 to promote your listing online. You are still an owner, and the property is for sale by you, the owner, now represented by an agent. Do not disguise this fact, and use only those listing sites that permit agent listings as well as FSBO listings.

Run classified ads that reference your own listing Web site or your agent's online listing of your home. Just remember not to represent the property as a FSBO and to refer any buyer prospects to your agent.

Promote the Co-Op Opportunity

Every listing agent lusts to sell his own listing to a buyer he has found (or who has found him). The listing agent lusts for the full commission rather than a 50/50 split on a co-op. In reality, the listing agent is not highly motivated to seek out a co-op sale. (This is an understatement.)

Remember:
You, as the seller, pay the same commission, whether the sale is a co-op or not. It is in your interest to promote the co-op opportunity to every agent and real estate office you can contact.

Take it upon yourself to promote your property to every local real estate office. Use your agent's flyer or your own and mail or fax it to every office you can—and do so each and every week. To find agents you can email, go to iOwn.com and pull up a list of agents within a 25-mile radius of your home by using the Agent Finder function. Start by going to the iOwn.com Selling Center at *www.iown.com/selling/index.htm* and then select AgentFinder to get to the query form. Here you can enter a city/state/radius search or a zip code search.

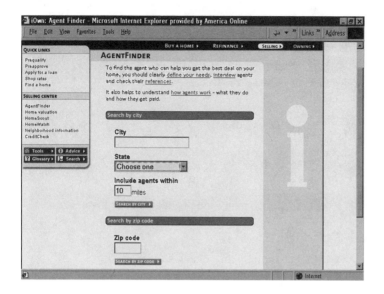

Fill out the iOwn.com search form to find agents in your area to whom you can send your listing agent's marketing materials.

You will get a list of dozens of agents, with email icons shown for each. As an example, the results of a search for agents within 25 miles of Phoenix, Arizona, are found in the following figure.

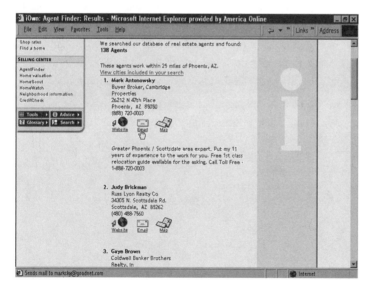

Search results for agents using iOwn.com. Note the email icon for each agent. It is not spamming to send an email to agents in your market area promoting your MLS listing.

Click the email icon to send your listing information to as many agents as you want. Note that what you are doing is *not* spamming. Your listing is in the MLS; you are notifying these local agents of your listing. Not a single agent will object to receiving your email.

Wrapping It Up

In this chapter, you learned the following:

- Reasons for listing your home with an agent

- How to evaluate agents and negotiate the listing agreement

- What a CMA is

- What a marketing plan *is* and what a plan *isn't*

- How to help your agent promote your property

The tone of this chapter has been negative about listing agents. The reason is to make you vigilant in your agent interview and evaluation process. There are many fine, ethical, professional real estate agents and brokers, but it can be difficult to find one amid all the hype and self-promotion agents indulge in. (Can you imagine *your* picture on a highway billboard?) Your job is to find one of these high-caliber professionals to list and sell your home quickly, at full market value, for a reasonable commission.

This is no small challenge, but at least you now have some guidance from the ideas in this chapter to help you in your quest.

PART III

Financing (or Re-Financing) Your Home Online

CHAPTER 7

Financing Your Dream Home

If you found your dream home online and now want to figure out how to buy it—or if you just want to know how much you can spend for your new home—you need to tap the mortgage resources available on the Net.

Mortgage information, calculations, and online applications are only a few clicks away, thanks to the rapid growth of online lending. From a few pioneers in 1996 to thousands of sources today, your choices for online mortgage research and origination are *virtually* (no pun intended) unlimited. Like most Net research, it's culling the wheat from the chaff that's the problem. We will begin navigating the maze by doing some basic research online. As we go, I'll be slipping in some jargon and referring you to the glossary in Appendix A for formal definitions.

Researching Mortgage Loans Online

A large sign hangs in a local print shop in my hometown. It says in bold red lettering:

LOW PRICE

HIGH QUALITY

FAST DELIVERY

(Pick any two)

Companies operating in cyberspace and offering products and services online seem to be promising all three of these benefits. If we find an online mortgage lender with the lowest rate, can we get the loan closed within our contractual time frame? Or do we

What You'll Learn in This Chapter:

▶ How to research mortgage rates online and how to comparison shop for mortgage loans

▶ More than you probably want to know about discount points and APR and the importance of using APR to compare lenders' loan costs

▶ Where to go for information on first-time home-buyer loan programs

▶ What sites to use to get lenders to bid for your loan business

▶ How tedious mortgage finance and research can be

risk losing our new home to another buyer because our low-priced online lender was swamped with applications and delayed processing and closing our loan?

These are legitimate questions. Instead of having a choice of a few dozen local lenders, we can choose from thousands. Diligence is required to find the one company that can live up to the cyberspace promise of "better, cheaper, and faster." One of the fantastic benefits of the Internet is the power it puts in our hands to find information we can use to our negotiating advantage. We can use the competitive information to apply leverage in our negotiations with local lenders if we choose. And we can be constantly on top of the rapidly changing interest rate picture. First, let's do a quick check of what interest rates are doing in general.

Finding Rate Information

Point your browser to the guru of all financial data, Bloomberg. Use this URL to go directly to the mortgage rate summary:

www.bloomberg.com/markets/rates.html

Here's a mortgage rate summary presented by Bloomberg.com. This is where you can quickly get a snapshot of current mortgage rates.

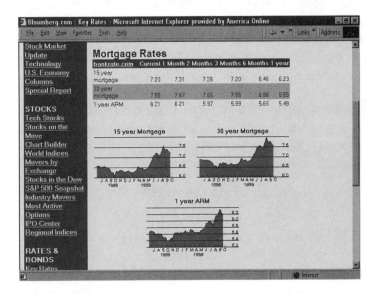

In late September 1999, this site shows that the 30-year fixed rate mortgage is 7.55 percent. The convenient chart shows that the low of 6.5 percent occurred almost exactly one year ago, in early October 1998. The trend has been steadily climbing to a peak of

8 percent (reached in mid-August 1999) and then down to the current level of 7.55 percent. Is this an actual rate? Is there a single national rate? Will my local lender have this rate? The answers are "No," "No," and "Maybe." Here's why.

Unlike products that may have a "manufacturer's suggested list price," there is no defined price for mortgages. They are like other commodities such as wheat and corn that are priced by supply and demand. There are prices in local markets for mortgages, and they vary among lenders, just as the price of corn varies slightly from one grocery store to another. There is no single national price for a mortgage. So when you see a rate on an online service such as Bloomberg.com, you are seeing an average of many lenders' rates across the country.

Without getting into the technicalities, there is a wholesale cost of mortgage money. By offering different rate and discount point combinations (more on this later), lenders mark up the price to a retail price—the rate for you, the consumer. Lenders compete locally on rates with other lenders licensed to do business in your state.

Rates are dynamic, changing daily and sometimes more than once per day, depending on the volatility in the financial markets. The short-term trend of mortgage rates can be tracked by the yield of 10-year and 30-year Treasury bonds. If bonds are down sharply in price and up in yield on a given day, you will find mortgage rates moving higher the next day. Refer back to the discussion in Chapter 1, "A Brief Overview of Real Estate in a Networked World," on "Monitoring Mortgage Rates."

What Are Rates and Points, Anyway?

To answer this question, we must understand the precise definitions for (jargon alert!) *rate*, *par*, and *discount point*. Nothing in mortgage lending confuses consumers more than interest rate and discount points. Everyone wants the lowest possible note rate for their mortgage, but few understand the complexities regarding note rate, permanent and temporary buydowns with discount points, par rate, and APR. So let me try to clear up the confusion.

When you have a mortgage loan with a specific fixed rate on the note, say 7.25 percent, and a fixed repayment period, say 30 years, we call that a *30-year fixed rate loan at 7.25 percent*. Neither the term nor the rate will change, nor will the level payment required each month ever change.

The total amount borrowed is called the *principal amount* of the loan, or the *face amount* of the note. The annual interest rate stated in the note is the note rate, the so-called *interest rate* of the loan.

This note rate is what we seek to minimize. You can get just about any rate you want. The figure that follows (from the iOwn.com Web site) is one lender's rate quote for a 30-year fixed loan. Looking at the figure, we can see that many rates are offered, each with a specific point/rebate and APR.

When we ask a lender to quote us a rate, what we first want to know is the par, or 0/0 rate. Par is the rate offered by the lender net of any up-front origination fee or discount points. So a par rate is quoted with zero origination points and zero discount points—0/0 for short. It is marginally useful for comparing rates among lenders. I say *marginally useful* because the lender may have other fees, such as an application fee or an extended lock fee, that are not included in the par rate quote. *Only an accurately calculated APR can be used for true rate comparison.* But I am getting ahead of the story.

Remember:

Your total housing payment is made up of your mortgage payment of principal and interest (which stays constant with a fixed-rate loan) and monthly tax, insurance, and possibly mortgage insurance payments that go into your escrow account. Your total housing payment may change as taxes and insurance rates change, but your fixed rate mortgage payment never changes.

What Is an Origination Fee?

An *origination fee* is a fee paid to the lender for making the loan. Normally, the loan officer's commission is paid from this fee. It is quoted in *points*. A point, in mortgage jargon, is 1 percent of the loan amount. This is the first and most significant cost incurred in getting a mortgage. Origination points vary by market and may range from .5 point to 1.5 points for conforming loans and up to 5 points or more for non-conforming subprime loans.

In the Midwest market, we charge a 1 percent origination fee, if we are quoting a below par rate. (More about this later.)

Because no company and no professional work for free, the origination fee will get paid either directly by the borrower as part of closing costs or indirectly through "premium" or rebate pricing.

What this means is that to quote a rate, called the *par* or *no-fee* rate, the lender specifies a slightly higher interest rate (usually about .25 percent more). When a loan with this rate is sold in the secondary market, the investor pays a rebate or *premium* back to the lender, equal to the lender's required origination fee.

Look at the various rate and point combinations in the following figure. These rates are offered by Flagstar, which is the lender in this example. Focus on the 7.375 percent and 7.75 percent rates and notice that the former has 1.625 points required and the latter requires 0.0 points, a difference of 1.625. What does this mean? Simply put, on a $100,000 loan, the 7.375 percent rate would require $1,625 paid at closing as an up-front interest fee; the 7.75 percent loan would require no extra payment. The 7.75 percent rate is the *par rate* in this example because it costs you no points to get a loan from Flagstar at that rate.

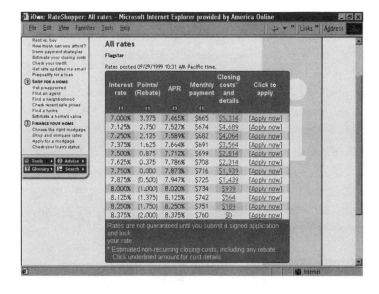

This rate-quote table for 30-year loans is from iOwn.com. We're looking at the rates available and the points we'd have to pay to get a loan at that rate.

Discount Points Defined and Explained

Let's suppose that you want a lower-than-par rate and are willing to pay for it. The lender will quote you various rates with discount points added.

What Are Discount Points?

Here's a working definition of *discount*: the amount an investor or lender requires to be paid in advance (either as an added amount or as a discount from face value) to make a given note rate yield the desired amount. One discount point is 1 percent of the loan amount.

What all this means to you as a consumer is that if you want the lowest rate possible, you pay discount points up front to the lender. (This is called permanently "buying" down the rate.) Therefore, when we compare rates, we want to compare both the interest rate and the points charged to get the given rate.

Points are shown either as positive amounts such as 1.25—which is a cost of 1.25 percent *in addition* to the normal closing costs— or as negative amounts, such as (1.25) or –1.25—which is a rebate amount that can *reduce* closing costs.

For example, Flagstar is offering a 7.875 percent rate with (.500) points and an 8.250 percent rate with (1.75) points. Both are rebate prices. The difference is 1.250 points, or $1,250 on a $100,000 loan. If we were short of funds and could accept the $26 per month higher payment at the 8.25 percent rate, we could apply the rebated $1,250 to the closing costs, to reduce our total funds to close. This rebate option can be helpful, especially if there is a good chance you'll be moving or refinancing the house in a few years. (Note that it would take 48 months at $26/month to recover $1,250.)

This brings us to APR, or annual percentage rate, a confusing concept to consumers but vitally important for rate comparison shopping—especially on the Internet.

Be Aware:

Brokers and loan officers can make money from rebate or premium pricing (also called *yield spread premium*) by not passing on the full rebate to you. This is not as likely to happen with online lenders as it is with local mortgage brokers because of the intense price competition on the Internet.

Annual Percentage Rate (APR)

To better protect consumers from being ravaged by banks and mortgage companies, federal regulations require lenders to disclose an *annual percentage rate*, or *APR*, in addition to the note rate.

The APR is defined and calculated in a way that is supposed to help consumers compare interest rate offers among lenders. Mostly, it confuses consumers. Because all loans are made with some costs charged to the borrower, APR was defined to include all required costs and reduce the loan amount to an *amount financed* figure on which the annual percentage rate calculation is made. This is best explained by example (see the following sidebar) and explained in plain English.

In mortgage lending, regulations define certain costs and fees as *finance charges* and require that they be deducted from the loan amount to get the *amount financed*. This amount is used in the amortization calculation rather than the note's face or principal amount to solve for interest rate. Because no loan is obtained without some cost, *the amount financed is always less than the principal* and *APR is always higher than note rate.*

What makes APR useful is that all lenders are supposed to calculate it in the same way, with the same costs included in the calculation, so that consumers can comparison shop lenders by APR. In reality, APR rarely works the way it was intended, because lenders have creative ways of using (or perhaps we should say, *ab*using) the APR calculation.

One brief example will help explain the use of APR in comparing rates. Consider a 30-year fixed rate of 7.375 percent with 1.590 points total cost. Consider another 30-year fixed rate of 7.625 percent with only .590 points. Which loan is the better deal?

Let's look at the APR calculations of these two rate offers:

Note Rate/Points	7.375% / 1.590	7.625% / .590
Loan Amount/Pmt	$100,000 / 691	$100,000 / 708
APR	7.705%	7.854%

It appears that the 7.375 percent rate is better based on APR; that is true for the life of the loan. Nevertheless, you'll be paying an additional 1.0 point, or $1,000, up front to save $17 in the monthly payment with the lower note rate. It would take almost 5 years (58 months) to recoup the $1,000. So even though APR can be useful, it is not the only factor to consider in comparing loans.

How to Compare Rates Online

If two or more lenders are offering identical rates, say 7.5 percent, you can compare them based on APR. The lower APR is better. Because the required cost of originating the loan is included in

---

Understanding APR

Suppose that you borrow $100 from me at 8 percent simple interest for one year. I charge you a $2 fee to make the loan. In effect, you get $98 but have to repay me $108 at the end of 1 year. You really financed only $98, because you got $100 minus the $2 fee. After a year, you paid $8 interest (8 percent of $100) on this $98. Because Rate = Interest ÷ Principle, your APR is 8.16 percent ($8/$98) on this simple interest loan.

Remember:

All confusion aside, APR is still the best comparison factor when comparing identical note rates among lenders.

the APR calculation, this is a reasonably good way to compare lenders—but only if you are comparing apples and apples. The terms and features of each loan (and the rate) should be identical for the APR to be a valid indicator.

One more example should clear up the issue. Go online to *www.mortgage101.com* and select Interest Rate Survey. From the next screen, choose a state. (Remember that rates are localized by state.) The screen you'll see is a list of quotes for a $125,000 conventional mortgage.

In this list of rate quotes for $125,000 loans from Mortgage101. com, can you find the best deal for a 7.5 percent loan?

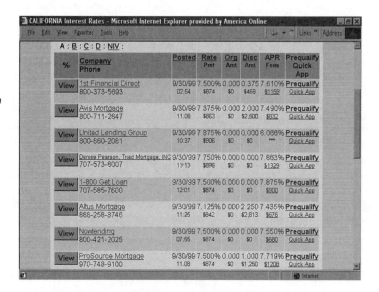

Can you spot the best deal for a 7.5 percent loan, based on APR? In the sample screen, there are four loans offered at 7.5 percent. Nowlending (the next-to-last one listed) has the lowest APR of the four. Study the four 7.5 percent offerings carefully and check the costs on each. Notice how much more in points and total costs you could pay with the three lenders with the higher APRs.

Where are the best places to go online for rate comparison shopping? Read on!

MortgageQuotes.com

The first stop on a tour of the best sites for rate comparison shopping is MortgageQuotes.com:

www.mortgagequotes.com

This site won't win any awards for graphic design, but what it lacks in visual appeal it makes up for in quality of information and speedy response. In addition to giving access to hundreds of lenders' rates, Microsurf, Inc., the parent company of this site, actually enforces honesty from the participating lenders who advertise their rates here. They purge lenders from their database who use "bait and switch" or "lowball" (artificially low) rate quotes. You will have to work to get the rate quotes from this site (they are four pages deep into the site), but the information is worth the effort.

Try It Yourself ▼

1. From the home page, select Today's Rates to get to the state selection screen.

2. Click your state to go to the loan category page for your state.

3. Choose from among these loan categories: Conforming, Jumbo, FHA, VA, or B, C, & D Credit Programs. Brief definitions are shown onscreen. Go ahead and select Conforming and get to the next (and final) screen, where you can select a loan program and point or cost preference.

4. Select the 30-year fixed rate, and you will see a result screen containing many lenders' rates.

5. Be sure to scroll down to see all of the lenders' rates.

▲

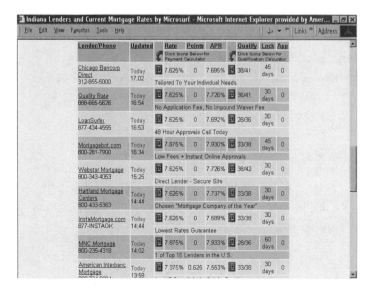

Rate quotations from advertising lenders on Microsurf's MortgageQuotes. com. The APRs are calculated by Microsurf to ensure consistency among lenders.

Use the APR to compare rates. Microsurf calculates the APRs from point and cost information supplied by each lender, to ensure accurate and uniform calculations. For additional information on a particular loan, you can go to the lender's site directly or call the listed telephone number. After you have found some attractive rates, print the page or pages with the best rates and then try the next site on our tour.

Interest.com

The next stop on our online tour of lenders is Interest.com:

> *www.interest.com*

From the menu list on the home page, choose Comparison Shop Mortgage Rates, then select a state (a process familiar to us by now). On the next screen, specify a loan type and amount. The result is a lengthy, unsorted list of lenders and rates.

The information Interest.com presents is complete; you can go directly to the lender's Web site to apply or get more information. However, this list is difficult to use online, because it is not sorted on rate or APR, and you can see only about four lenders per screen before you have to scroll down again. You'll need to print out the results and study them with a highlighter in hand.

Find your best three or four lenders here, then move on to our final stop.

Mortgage101.com

We have seen Mortgage101.com before, earlier in this chapter. Take another look at their rate comparisons by going to this site:

> *www.mortgage101.com*

From the opening page, you are just two clicks away from a long and well-organized list of lenders. If you minimize your toolbars and set your browser's fonts to Smallest, you can get 9 or 10 loans displayed per page.

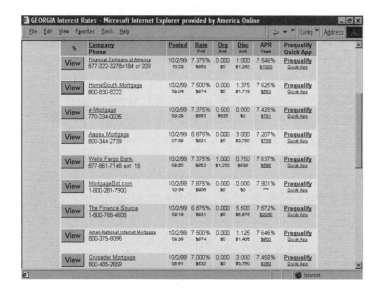

A listing of lenders and rates from Mortgage101.com for the state of Georgia. Remember that rates may vary by state.

From the line item listing, click the VIEW button to open another browser window to show additional rates from the lender selected, a very useful feature. As was true with the Interest.com site, the Mortgage101.com site does not sort the results, and some lenders are seen multiple times, with different rates in different positions in the listings. Nonetheless, this list, which is best printed out, gives you a great selection of lenders to peruse by rate, points, and APR. Keep your yellow highlighter handy for marking the best lender choices; we still have more research to do.

Online Loan Origination Resources

We have shopped some rates and have found a few lenders that could be possible choices for our next mortgage. Let's expand our search to include the major broker and *referral* (or *aggregator*) sites. Then we'll review the national online direct lenders. (Hang in there, we only have 10 more sites to visit!)

Broker and Referral Sites

Mortgage brokers take applications for loans and submit them to wholesale lenders for funding. The brokers are compensated by fees charged or by a rebate from the lender called the *yield spread premium*. Referral sites (sometimes called *aggregators*), such as

Quicken and HomeAdvisor, have relationships with lenders that you select from their sites based on rate, cost, and terms. You apply directly to the chosen lender, and the referring site is paid a fee by the lender (which should always be disclosed to you).

We will look at two referral sites, Quicken Mortgage and HomeAdvisor, and then at one broker site, iOwn.com. These and the sites just covered are the cream of the crop. There are plenty of other broker and referral sites, but these three are all you need to wrap up your diligent comparison shopping. (We can't spend the new millennium just surfing mortgage sites—there are so many, you could spend years just looking at them all.)

The Quicken.com Referral Site

Quicken Mortgage, brought to you by the folks at Intuit who developed the best-selling Quicken personal finance software, is a referral site with many useful features, including the ability to quickly shop rates among their associated lenders. Quicken offers a choice of least 15 lenders in each state (none in Rhode Island, however). Go directly to their home page with this direct link:

http://mortgage.quicken.com

From the navigation panel on the left, select Quick Rates. You will have to fill in state and loan information on the form and then submit it to get a summary. The list is sorted by ascending APR, which is helpful because the lowest-cost loan for a given rate appears first. No need for the printed copy or highlighter here.

Getting more information from this point on is awkward and time consuming. You have to register and input information across several screens to get through the pre-qualifying interview process. When you are finally finished (if you have the patience), you will see a selection of loans that you qualify for.

Don't Waste Your Time:

Don't waste your time with Quicken's convoluted "interview" unless the Quick Rate survey found you a killer rate.

The HomeAdvisor Referral Site

Point your browser to Microsoft Network's HomeAdvisor site by typing in this link:

http://homeadvisor.msn.com

From the top-left of the screen, select Shop for Rates. With one click, you'll get rates from 10 affiliated lenders for California (don't we all live in California?). You can then select your state, loan amount, and the points you want to pay to get an updated quote from lenders in your state. The results are unsorted, so you should print them out and see how they compare with your previous research.

Now let's try a top-of-the-line broker site and finish up our window shopping (no pun intended) for rates.

The iOwn.com Broker Site

Under Shop Rates on the left side of the main page, select your state (if you don't live in California), and then hit the Search button. The resulting page, shown in the following figure, gives you the top 10 lenders' rates, sorted by APR within rate, which is the most efficient presentation we've seen yet. (You can also click a lender to see all the rates offered by that lender.)

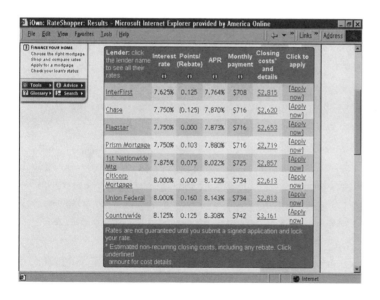

Here's a lender summary from iOwn.com. Additional rates from each lender are only a click away.

If you scroll down the search results page, you can tailor your search more precisely by specifying additional loan parameters. You can search for the lowest APR, the lowest total costs, desired points, or a specified rate. This is a good place to take your previous research and compare it against the lenders available through iOwn. Make sure that you compare using the same assumptions and characteristics for each loan.

By now, you should have a short list of lenders with excellent rates and loan programs. It's time to see how our research compares to the direct online lenders (the ones who only lend in cyberspace).

National Online Lender Sites

Now we'll turn to the national online mortgage banking sites that tout their Web-based origination service. We will shop these sites to see how they stack up against what our research has uncovered so far. Each of these online lenders lets you apply and get approval online, at your leisure, without ever schlepping down to some office with your stack of documentation. (In fact, there *aren't* any branch offices for you to go to.) With these outfits, you go into serious debt with a few keystrokes and mouse clicks and by mailing in some paperwork. Scary, isn't it? (In Chapter 8, "Applying for Your Mortgage Online," we will walk through an online application with several of these lenders to see the whole process.)

There is no preference implied by the order of presentation in these sites. You be the judge of the offerings of each site as we continue shopping for the best mortgage deals.

No more handholding, now you are on your own to check out each of these online lenders. My suggestion is that you go to each site with the same loan requirements. For example, shop for a 30-year fixed-rate loan of $120,000 on an assumed purchase price of $150,000 with a 30-day lock period, with a cost not to exceed 1 discount point.

As you proceed with your analysis, keep in mind the total range of services provided by the online lender. If two lenders seem to be tied on price, you will want to consider service, accessibility, and reputation. Responsiveness, both online and on the telephone, is another important factor in making your decision.

E-LOAN (www.eloan.com)

E-LOAN is one of the online mortgage pioneers. Launched in June 1997 from the transformation of Palo Alto Funding Group, a traditional mortgage brokerage, E-LOAN has grown to become one of the leading online mortgage bankers/brokers, with access to more than 70 lenders and a complete product line of loan programs. In addition to purchase money mortgages, refinancing options, and home equity loans, you can get a car loan (or refinance your current one) online with E-LOAN.

Start from the home page with the Finance Your Home Purchase link, which shows the special services and features E-LOAN offers and lets you search for rates by type of loan program.

Keystroke Financial, Inc. (www.keystroke.com)

Another Internet mortgage pioneer, Keystroke.com was originating loans online as early as February 1996. Through an online branch affiliation with Pacific Guarantee Mortgage, one of the largest national mortgage brokers, Keystroke can offer loans from a selection of over 200 lenders. Begin on the start page with the Search for the Best Rate button to check out their offerings.

Mortgage.com (www.mortgage.com)

Florida-based online mortgage banker Mortgage.com was founded in 1994 as First Mortgage Network. This company offers a full range of mortgage products to consumers and also provides technology to the industry. They fund $2 billion in loans annually; as mortgage bankers, they fund loans directly.

Begin your evaluation of this lender by clicking the RATES tab at the top of the home page.

Interloan.com (www.interloan.com)

Interloan, founded in 1977, is a subsidiary of a public company, Finet Holdings, Inc., which also owns Monument Mortgage, a California mortgage bank. This conventional lender (no FHA or VA online yet) has affiliations with some of the leading correspondent lenders and offers direct lending and full service options (through professional loan consultants) at discounted rates.

Interloan.com, a direct online lender, offers support from professional loan consultants in an effort to combine the traditional and the online lending experiences.

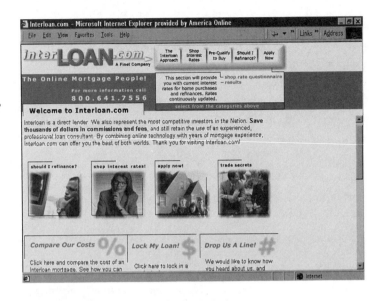

Start by clicking the Shop Interest Rates! button above the picture. You can also use the buttons at the top of the screen for navigation. Each button has a drop-down menu of selections.

Mouse Carefully

If you don't position your mouse pointer carefully and inadvertently click a blank part of Interloan's menu system, you will get an error.

Because each applicant has access to an experienced loan officer, the Interloan approach attempts to combine the best of two worlds: high-tech, online loan origination and traditional personalized mortgage banking.

At this time, you have exhaustively researched the major players in the online mortgage business. You should have a short list of companies you would consider dealing with online for originating your mortgage. But what if you are still just a little uncomfortable dealing with a company whose only existence seems to be in cyberspace? You might want to look closer to home.

Finding Local Lenders

The best mortgage lender for your unique situation could be right in your own city. It could be the mortgage division of your local bank or credit union. Local lenders can be very competitive on short maturity loans like ARMs and 3- and 5-year balloon mortgages. Sometimes they are competitive on the 15-year and

30-year fixed rate products, but you'll probably do better with the big online lenders or brokers for those long-term loans.

After you have done your online homework and have found some competitive rates and terms on a mortgage, call a few local banks and mortgage companies and get their quotes—or try to find them online.

Finding a local lender with an online rate quote or origination capability requires careful and precise query techniques on the various search engines. (You can also use Interest.com and Mortgage101.com to get lists of lenders licensed to do business in your state.) If any of the big national mortgage banks such as CountryWide, Norwest, North American, or Cendant has a branch office in your city, give them a call or go to their corporate Web site (see Appendix B, "Recommended Real Estate and Mortgage Web Sites") and link to a local branch. You can also try the mortgage divisions of some of the megabanks: NationsBank, First Union, Citibank, and BankOne.

Remember:
If you belong to a credit union that offers mortgages, be sure to check their rates and programs. Credit union mortgage products are usually limited to just a few conventional loans, but you might find a competitive rate with low closing costs.

Finding Programs for First-Time Homebuyers

Most of the lenders we have visited so far are competing for the experienced homebuyer with excellent credit and the ability to make a down payment of 5 to 20 percent, and who will be borrowing $100,000 or more with a conventional loan. This is the easiest and most profitable high-volume business niche. Some of these lenders offer FHA and VA loans, and you should check them for rates, along with rates on 3-percent down conventional loans (which are used by many first-time homebuyers).

If you have difficulty finding an appropriate lender or loan program among the lenders covered earlier in this chapter, or if you want more information about lenders who specialize in government-insured loans (FHA, VA, RHS) or in special programs for first-time homebuyers, check out the sites shown in Table 7.1.

Table 7.1   Loan Information Links for First-Time Homebuyers

www.fanniemae.com/ singlefamily/products/ markets/emerging_markets.html	Direct link to Fannie Mae's products of interest to first-time homebuyers.
www.homepath.com	Get a list of lenders for Fannie Mae's products in your state.
www.freddiemac.com/sell/ expmkts/98online.html	Direct link to Freddie Mac's first-time homebuyer product line.
www.homesteps.com	Freddie Mac's site for sales of foreclosed properties with special financing for first-time homebuyers.
www.fhatoday.com	Online FHA lender site where you can learn about and apply for an FHA loan.
www.vba.va.gov/bln/loan/ LGYINFO.HTM	If you are a veteran, go straight into the VA's loan information area with this link. (If the link fails, start with *www.va.gov* and go to Benefits).
www.hud.gov/buyhome.html	HUD's extensive information for first-time homebuyers is located here.
www.hud.gov/mortprog.html	Direct link to information about federally insured mortgage programs, including FHA mortgages.
www.nehemiahprogram.com	Go here for information on the Nehemiah down payment gift program and to find a participating lender.

Mortgage Auctions: Bidding for Your Business

The final set of mortgage resources in this chapter is the so-called *auction sites*. These are not really online auctions in the eBay style, they are more of a bid-quotation system. You put your loan requirements online for lenders to evaluate, and they make an offer to you for a specific rate and cost for your mortgage. This is always a two-step process: You submit your information online, and lenders review your profile and requirements and respond to you with specific loan program offers, online or offline. You can then pick and choose among the offers to select the best one.

There are two primary reasons for using the services of these sites. The first is to verify your own research with online lenders and to possibly find a better deal than you found on your own.

If you have excellent credit and are looking for a conventional loan (under $240,000), you'll probably find that the auction approach will get you about the same results as the major online lenders. Still, this approach is worth a try.

The second reason to use the bid-quote sites is if your situation is unique in some way or if you need a jumbo (over $240,000) loan. (Lenders love jumbo loans and will compete vigorously for your jumbo business.) If your circumstances or loan program requirements are nonstandard (or nonconforming), you should use these sites. Suppose that you have blemished credit and unverifiable income and require a so-called "no income verification" loan. This is a non-conforming scenario, and you will do well to let these lenders quote for you.

Here are four excellent sites. Each of them offers to provide four or five quotes from lenders with no cost or obligation on your part. These are free services, so how can you lose?

- **LendingTree.com** (*www.lendingtree.com*)   This site promises up to four loan offers online within two business days of receiving your online information.

- **LoanWeb** (*www.loanweb.com*)   Similar to LendingTree, LoanWeb will get you lenders' quotes on mortgage loans, car loans, and credit cards.

- **RealEstate.com's Mortgage Auction** (*www.mortgageauction.com*)   This service will submit your mortgage requirements to over 250 lenders and notify you within 24 hours by email of the winning bidder.

- **Computer Loan Network** (*www.clnet.com*)   CLN puts your loan request on a mortgage multiple listing service, where interested lenders can find your request and respond directly to you by your choice of telephone, fax, or email.

Wrapping It Up

In this chapter, you have learned

- How to research mortgage rates online

- How to comparison shop for mortgage loans and which sites to shop

- More than you probably wanted to know about discount points and APR and the importance of using APR to compare lenders' loan costs

- Where to go for information on first-time homebuyer programs

- What sites to use to get lenders to bid for your loan business

- How tedious mortgage research can be

Thanks for your perseverance through all this! Take a well-earned break before we learn how to apply for a mortgage online.

CHAPTER 8

Applying for Your Mortgage Online

In this chapter, we are going to work through an online loan application with several lenders to help you understand the process and learn what to expect. In doing so, we will discover what information and documents we need and how easy an online, do-it-yourself mortgage loan application can be.

After this exercise, we'll review the approval and closing process so that you will understand the complete loan transaction from application to closing.

Working Through an Online Application

Before going online to apply for a mortgage, let's get organized. This is sort of like doing your income taxes: First you gather and organize your records, curse how disorganized you and your financial records are, and then promise yourself you'll get better organized.

What Information You Need to Supply

Every lender requires certain information to process and underwrite your loan. The information and its documentation fall into four categories as shown in Table 8.1. You will need to gather the documents and have the information handy when you go online.

What You'll Learn in This Chapter:

- ▶ How to apply for a mortgage online
- ▶ The kinds of documentation you'll have to supply to get a loan
- ▶ About conditional and final approval
- ▶ How the loan closing process works

Table 8.1   Typical Information and Documentation Needed for a Mortgage Application

Information Required	Documentation Needed
Personal information, including employment and income for all borrowers	Social Security numbers, employers' addresses, pay stubs for one month's pay history; W2s from prior two years; most recent two years' tax returns if you are self-employed; proof of child support payments if received
Credit information	Provided by credit bureaus (ordered by lender)
Personal assets and liabilities	Bank statements for checking and savings accounts; brokerage, mutual fund, and 401(k) statements; cash value of life insurance; market value, liens, and rents on investment property owned; landlord information if you are renting; summary of revolving and installment debt totals and monthly minimum payments
Information about the property you are purchasing	Purchase agreement or contract of sale; appraisal (will be ordered by lender)

You won't necessarily need all the documentation listed, but you should be prepared to provide it if the lender requests it. Don't try the old excuse "my records are already packed up and in storage." You'll end up unpacking boxes to get those W2 forms or tax returns if the lender wants them, or you simply won't get your loan approved.

Now let's see what it takes to do an application online.

From One Who Knows:

Mortgage lenders are worse than IRS auditors when it comes to acceptable documentation. If a loan officer or underwriter requests a specific document needed to approve your loan, you will *have* to provide it.

How Online Applications Are Taken

We are going to take a quick look at how two of the major online lenders have you do an online application. Although the information required from you is essentially the same for both sites, these two lenders approach the process of gathering your data in significantly different ways.

First, let's assume that during your research in the preceding chapter, you determined that E-LOAN had the best rates and options for your particular loan requirements. Here is what the application process would be like.

The E-LOAN Approach

With E-LOAN (*www.eloan.com*), you start with a brief introductory screen and then jump right to a linear, screen-by-screen input process that starts with basic personal information. You continue to input information until you complete the application process. The input screens are simple and easy to understand and complete.

The straight-through-to-completion approach required by E-LOAN is fine—unless your online session is interrupted or you want to go back and check a previous screen. If that happens, you'll have to start over from the beginning. Plan to work continuously and steadily through this application-input process.

There is nothing wrong with this straight-through process as long as you understand from the outset that you need to complete it in one continuous session. The online mortgage market is intensely competitive, and lenders are continually improving their user friendliness and services. By the time you read this, E-LOAN will probably have a "save and restore" capability implemented on its site.

Let's look now at a somewhat different application process from another lender. If, during your diligent search for the best rates and loan programs, you decided on mortgage.com's offering, here's how you would go about applying with them.

mortgage.com—Another Way to Apply

When you start an application at mortgage.com (*www.mortgage.com*) by selecting the Apply tab, you are taken to a comprehensive instruction page that gives you important information about the application process you are about to begin. There's a Progress heading on the left side; the bullets start out red and then turn green when you complete a section. You can save and quit at any time and return to pick up where you left off. You can review previous sections and make changes if necessary.

The next page asks for a username and a password you will use if you have to leave the site and then return during the application process.

After the setup, you start with the property and personal information form. You continue by inputting information for each of the sections for income, assets, debts, and so forth. Each input page is self-explanatory, and additional help is available by clicking the Help button. You should have no trouble moving right through the application-input forms.

The application process at mortgage.com is fairly straightforward, and you can always save what you've done and return to the application later.

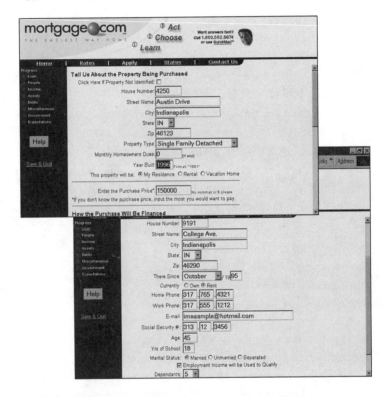

If you need to stop the application process (either from boredom or to find that missing bank statement), just click Save and Quit. You will get a choice of how you want to return: automatically (mortgage.com will recognize your computer) or by entering your username and password.

With both E-LOAN and mortgage.com, after you have completed all the input, you have an option to submit the application at that time, abandon the application, or submit it later. If you like, you can practice with dummy information just to get the feel of how the application process works. Now that you've read this far, you probably won't need to do so, because we're about to walk through a complete application.

Applying Online: A Step-by-Step Example

Assume that you have searched and shopped rates as we learned to do in Chapter 7, "Financing Your Dream Home," and decided to apply to iOwn.com (*www.iown.com*) based on the loan you found there. What we are going to do now is go step-by-step and see exactly what is required to do a complete online loan application.

1. After you click the Apply button for the chosen loan with iOwn.com, you'll go to the introductory mortgage application page. Note that iOwn.com saves your information as you proceed so that you can stop and return if necessary. You can review the documents iOwn.com suggests you have ready and then move on by clicking the Apply Now button.

   Try It Yourself ▼

2. Type a username and password to set up your login information (so that later you can access and update your application or check its status). Then you begin a seven-section application procedure. Only the first three sections are lengthy; the last four move very quickly. You can stop at any time and return to pick up where you left off, a handy feature indeed.

3. In Part 1 of 7, you enter personal information about yourself and your co-borrower, if there is one. You're asked for your name, birth date, marital status, whether you're applying by yourself or with someone else, number of dependents, address (and whether you currently own or rent), and contact information.

   There is nothing difficult here. You should be aware that your answers are becoming part of a legal document. The application is subject to federal loan fraud statutes (Title 18, US Code, Section 1001); you will eventually sign a "true and correct" certification. This is the time, as they say in court, for "the truth, the whole truth, and nothing but the truth."

   A Word to the Wise:
   Save yourself a world of hurt—don't shade the truth or make any misrepresentations on your loan application.

4. Part 2 of 7 is the employment and income section. The information you provide here is pretty straightforward. If you have a co-borrower, you will input his or her information in this part of the form as well. Conforming loans require a two-year

job history, so if you have not been employed with the same employer for two years, you will be asked to provide prior employment information. Our sample applicant (cleverly named Ima Sample) has been on his job at General Motors for 20 years, so no prior job history is needed.

In the income information area of this part of the form, notice that you can specify overtime, bonus, and commission income in addition to salary or wage information. If you are going to use overtime pay to qualify, you must have a two-year history of overtime pay reflected on your W2 forms, in addition to your regular wages. Don't qualify by using over-time income if you can avoid it; lenders don't like it because of the risk of discontinuance. It's also just common sense not to increase your obligations to the point of having to have the overtime pay just to meet them.

Remember:

Conforming loans—those purchased by the agencies—have strict guidelines; you'll be following those rules when you apply online. Nonconforming loans have widely varying guidelines, depending on the type of loan.

Part 2 of 7 of the iOwn.com online loan application asks for employment and salary history. Don't rely on bonuses and overtime pay, unless you have a two-year history of receiving this extra income.

FYI:

If you receive more than 25 percent of your annual income as commission or bonus income and you will be using that income to qualify, you will need to supply two years of tax returns for income verification, just as you would if you were self-employed.

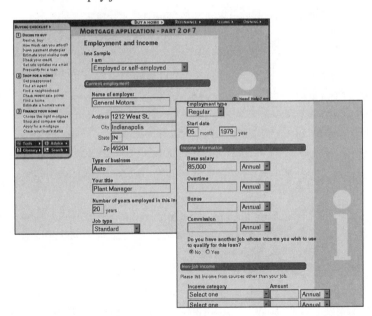

Notes for the Self-Employed:

If you are self-employed and minimize your taxable income by various write-offs, you have a dilemma when applying for a mortgage. Unless you apply for a *no income verification* (NIV) loan, you will have to supply your tax returns to the lender for self-employed income analysis. Here's the catch: Lenders look at your cash flow income based on your adjusted gross income from your tax return, with amounts added back for depreciation, extraordinary expenses, bad debt write-offs, and other items. These adjustments rarely compensate for the large (and sometimes creative) expense deductions most self-employed people take on their Schedule C or through their Sub-S or limited liability corporations.

This natural tendency to minimize taxable income for self-employed borrowers can sometimes force you into the NIV loan realm, where you will pay a higher interest rate in exchange for stating your income with no documentation required. Things sort of balance out if you are a self-employed borrower with low taxable income. What you save in income tax you tend to pay out in higher mortgage payments on the higher-interest rates charged for NIV loans.

5. Part 3 of 7 of the application form requests information about your financial and other assets. In the first part of the form, you enter the estimated value of any automobiles you own (or own with your bank). Do not enter anything for leased vehicles. Estimate a value for your personal property and household goods. This can be a guess or a value based on what you have your possessions insured for.

You also have to enter information about your financial accounts, including stocks, mutual funds, and 401(k) accounts. Enter enough assets to prove that you can make the down payment, pay the closing costs, and still have two months' mortgage payments in reserve. If you are a high-income earner ($100,000 per year or more), show enough assets to prove financial responsibility commensurate with your income. If you make $150,000 per year, for example, and have only $1,500 in your checking account and a few thousand in mutual funds, an underwriter might wonder why your assets are so low relative to your income. This disparity of income versus assets usually happens when there are undisclosed debts, mortgages, or perhaps a profligate life style (gambling or drugs). You don't want to appear unsavory, so show enough assets (assuming, of course, that you have them to disclose).

If you own other real estate, investment property, or a second home, you'll have some additional information to provide on another form. When you are finished entering the asset information, the remaining input sections are routine and go very quickly.

Tax Liens and Student Loans:

Tax liens must be paid off and student loans must be brought current to get a mortgage.

Notice that you have not been asked to enter any information about your debts, such as car loans and credit cards. That information will be merged into your application when the credit report is run. You authorize the credit report in Part 6.

6. Part 4 of 7 is the easiest form of all, the so-called legal declarations. You can answer most of the questions asked in this part of the form by clicking the Yes and No radio buttons.

If you've had a bankruptcy within the past seven years, say so here. Your credit report carries your bankruptcy history for 10 years, but if it has been discharged for more than seven years, you can answer No on this form. Be sure to disclose child support obligations here—they figure into your debt ratio. If you have ever had a foreclosure or deed-in-lieu of foreclosure (see the Glossary in Appendix A), you will have to explain the circumstances in detail. Likewise, if you have any current tax liens or a defaulted student loan, you will have to explain it here. After you answer these questions, you're through with the hard parts of the application.

Part 4 of 7 of the iOwn.com online loan application concerns the legal declarations you have to make. Answer honestly; you will be found out if you don't.

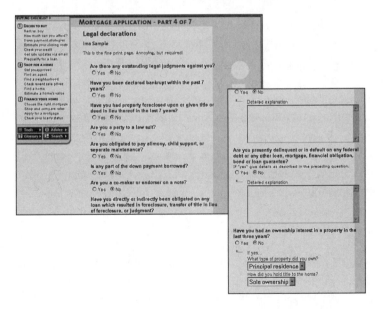

7. In Part 5 of 7 of the online application, you are asked some questions about the purpose of the loan, the loan amount, the value of the property, and occupancy and title preferences.

You also enter the address of the property if you have already offered a purchase agreement. Although you do not have to identify a property when you apply for a loan, you do have to specify a loan amount and the estimated purchase price before the lender will issue an approval commitment.

8. When you move on to Part 6 of the application, the only information required is your Social Security number (and that of your co-borrower, if there is one). When you click the Next button, you are authorizing the lender to access your credit report. You will have a final option to submit or abandon the application when we finish Part 7, so clicking the Next button here does not cause a credit report to be run at this point in the application process.

9. Part 7 of the application is the mortgage search form, which you would have used before you started the application. This is just another opportunity to check rates and confirm your loan selection. iOwn.com does not hold you to this choice; you can change loan programs later, until you are ready to lock in your rate.

10. After you select a loan and click the Next button, you are finished. A final Review and Update page is displayed. Here you have a color-coded list of the seven parts you have completed. If any items remain incomplete, you can go back and edit the parts required until you have all "green lights." You can then submit the application with a final click.

Because we are not yet in a paperless world, your online lender will send you an application package containing the application and various disclosure forms, along with your good faith estimate of closing costs and a truth-in-lending disclosure containing the calculated APR. You will sign and return these documents, along with your other documents (pay stubs, W2 forms, and so on) to formally begin the loan processing and underwriting cycle.

The better online lenders have a single person assigned to your loan as your contact for questions, for status information, and for coordinating the closing with the title company or attorney.

Approval and Closing with an Online Lender

What should you expect after submitting your application to an online lender? The process of approval and closing is similar to that required if you apply to a bricks and mortar lender instead of one in cyberspace. You will have to supply needed documents by overnight courier service if you're in a time pinch rather than by dropping them off at an office. You'll use the telephone and fax machine repeatedly, but you'd do that with a local lender as well.

Communication is important. You want a lender with a loan officer, consultant, or customer service representative (CSR) who is responsive by telephone, fax, or email. Responsiveness is the essential service issue as closing day approaches. So what happens?

Conditional Approval

After all the documentation is in order, your lender's underwriter (which may be a computer) will give you a preliminary or conditional approval. There will probably be several conditions or stipulations to be satisfied before you get final approval and can close the loan.

What sort of conditions should you expect? Some are simple document requests, such as a most recent pay stub or bank statement. Other conditions can be more complicated to satisfy.

Conditions to satisfy underwriters before final approval can include the following:

- Lender- or investor-required documents that are missing or out of date from the original application

- Resolution of credit issues, such as paying off a collection or judgement or providing a written explanation of their existence

- Proof of sufficient funds to close

- Proof of hazard insurance

- Title or property issues, such as an appraisal or survey exception

- Satisfactory required inspections, such as a termite inspection

If the appraisal has not been completed, a satisfactory appraisal will *always* be one of the conditions of the loan. If the appraisal has been completed but requires a repair or notes a significant defect in the property (such as a structural defect), resolution of the condition may be more difficult and time-consuming than you would like.

Most conditions are simple documentation issues and can be readily handled. Don't even think about trying to avoid supplying what the underwriter requests; you'll lose the argument every time. Just give them what they want as quickly as possible, accept the hassle, and save yourself a lot of grief.

Forewarned Is Forearmed: Underwriters are stubborn beyond comprehension. They can prevent your loan from closing on schedule if you don't give them the %#@x#& pay stub, credit explanation letter, or whatever it is they want. Give them what they want as quickly as you can.

Final Approval

After all the conditions have been met and the underwriter signs off on your loan, you will have final approval. This means that you can now close the transaction with a title company or attorney, as your state requires. The mortgage lender will supply the necessary documents and funds to the closing agent in time for the scheduled closing.

The Closing Process

If all has gone well and you have final loan approval from your online lender, the lender will send a closing package to the closing attorney or title company a day or two before your closing or settlement date. This package will contain the loan documents and a check for the mortgage amount, less any lender closing fees you or the sellers are paying. The title search and title insurance policy will have been completed, as will a survey. The closing office will prepare a new deed to the property in your name.

Funds to Close: Show Me the Money

You will come to the closing or settlement meeting with your cashier's check for your funds to close. *Funds to close* include your down payment and your portion of closing costs, minus your earnest money deposit and other prepaid fees. You will be given credit on the settlement statement for all your paid-in-advance items, such as the appraisal and credit report fees.

**How Much
Money?**
The settlement state-
ment specifies the
exact amount of
money you must
bring to closing in
the form of a certi-
fied check. If there
are adjustments at
the closing table,
minor shortages can
be paid by personal
check; any excess
funds will be
refunded.

By regulation, your attorney or title company must provide you with a copy of the settlement statement 24 hours before settlement for you to review. Insist on seeing a copy before closing so that you can review it with your loan officer over the telephone and compare it to your good faith estimate.

Buyer and Seller Responsibilities

At settlement, the buyer has the responsibility to deliver the property to you in the same condition as when your offer to purchase was accepted. It must be delivered with a marketable, insured title, free of any liens or other encumbrances. Shortly before closing, you and your real estate agent, if any, will walk through the home to verify the condition before you go to the closing.

Always Do a Walk-through Before Closing

Sellers are frequently stressed and sometimes angry about selling, moving, and meeting the contracted closing date. Terms and conditions in the original sales agreement may be forgotten, ignored, or violated. I have seen cases in which the seller removed light fixtures and replaced them with cheaper ones. In one case, the seller removed a big new refrigerator and replaced it with a smaller, used one. This deception failed because the buyer refused to close after the walkthrough until the refrigerator was returned. Sellers sometimes do petty things like removing all the light bulbs. You have a contractual agreement; make the seller comply with every condition.

In some markets, it may be "standard procedure" for the buyer to take possession of the property 30 days after closing. As you can imagine, this is a great risk to the buyer and a free ride for the seller. In other markets, the seller has to lease the property back after closing if he can't give possession at closing. Try to negotiate possession at closing.

Around the closing table, the documents will be explained by the closing attorney or escrow agent and then signed. The first document normally reviewed and signed by buyer and seller is the HUD-1 Settlement Statement. This uniform document is used in every state to account for the disbursement of funds and to itemize fees and the details of the transaction.

As the borrower, you will do most of the signing, because there are numerous loan documents to sign, including the promissory note and mortgage. After all the papers are signed and the money changes hands, you are a homeowner and a mortgagor. Your lender is the mortgagee. Your debt is secured by your new home.

Wrapping It Up

After working through this chapter, you should now know the following:

- How to complete an online lender's application
- What documentation you'll need to complete a loan application
- What to expect at conditional and final loan approval
- What happens at the closing

Gee. You did all this online, from the comfort of your current home, when it was convenient for you. Imagine that! You went more than a hundred thousand dollars in debt while sitting around the house in your underwear.

PART IV

Use the Internet to Find Bargain and Investment Property

CHAPTER 9

How to Find Bargain Properties Online

Beginning with this chapter, we focus on real estate as an investment. As with any asset you invest in, you want to buy low and sell high. Because the carrying costs of real estate are substantial (taxes, maintenance, debt service), if you buy to resell real estate rather than to hold it for rental income, you must buy *well below* the market to make an acceptable profit. You also want a reasonable rate of return on your invested capital in return for the risk you take.

If you invest $10,000 in the stock market, you have no carrying cost of the investment, other than the foregone return on a totally safe investment in government bonds. You can also cut your losses quickly if the investment sours. If you buy a piece of investment real estate with $10,000 down and a $90,000 mortgage, you had better know what you're doing. Many fortunes have been made in real estate, and many of those fortunes have been lost in bankruptcy court.

The bottom line is this for buying and reselling real estate: You want to buy "wholesale" and sell "retail." With interest rates above 8 percent for mortgages on investment property, when you buy to hold for rental income, you still need to buy at wholesale. Rental property purchased at market price is not much of an investment with interest rates where they are relative to rents.

As an investor, you'll find the information in this chapter valuable in helping you locate bargain-priced properties. And if you are a homebuyer looking for great deal in a personal residence, albeit one that may need rehabilitation, this chapter is useful reading for you as well.

What You'll Learn in This Chapter:

▶ How to search for and find "distressed" properties

▶ Where to get foreclosure information

▶ How to find bank-owned properties

▶ What the government agencies have to offer

New to Real Estate Investing?

The discussion from here on assumes that you are currently a real estate investor or that you are somewhat knowledgeable about real estate. If you are a "newbie" to real estate investing, you'll be spending some time in the Appendix A of this book, the glossary. We are not going to slow down to explain every detail. There's money waiting to be made!

One thing to keep in mind if you are a first-time homebuyer or a trade-up buyer: What may be a bargain for an investor may be a nightmare for you as a homeowner. (There will be more said about the nightmare scenario later.)

In this chapter, we are going to look for bargain residential properties online. For our purposes, these properties are classified into two categories: distressed and foreclosed. Let's begin with the distressed category and then move on to the foreclosures and bank-owned properties. One caveat: We are interested only in one- to four-family residential properties. These are the easiest to find, finance, and resell; they are also the lowest-risk category for investors. Multifamily and commercial real estate investing is another ballgame and beyond the scope of this book.

Finding Distressed Properties Online

For our discussion, a *distressed property* is a property that can be purchased below market value either because of needed rehabilitation or because the seller is in financial difficulty and must sell below market value to sell quickly (or a combination of these two situations). A home in good repair, priced at fair market value, in a reasonable location will eventually sell near fair market when demand (which occurs over time) is adequate. Some sellers can't wait for demand to clear the market. They are distressed and must sell below market price, where the demand will be greater.

In sum, we want to look for distressed one-to-four–unit residential properties, distressed sellers of the same, or both. Where can we go on the Internet to find these potential real estate bargains?

Distressed FSBOs Are Everywhere

A property listed by a real estate agent is, by definition, less distressed than one offered for sale by owner. This is not true in every case, but we want the most bang for our buck, so we'll start with distressed FSBO properties.

Where do we look for these properties and sellers? Not on the major pay-for-listing FSBO sites covered in Chapter 4, " How to Find the Perfect FSBO Property," and Chapter 5, "Sell Your Home Yourself and Save Thousands." Those sites are great for prime properties, but we're not likely to find many distressed properties or distressed sellers. There are exceptions to this rule, of course, and the best FSBO site to consider for distressed properties is *www.owners.com*, because it is the biggest FSBO site and offers free listings with a picture.

Let's go online and see what we find. Throughout this and the examples that follow, we are going to search for bargain properties in the metropolitan area I am most familiar with: Indianapolis. Real estate investing should be done close to home in the market area you know best. (Several investors I know never buy properties more than a 30-minute drive from their personal homes.)

Assume that you have $10,000 to invest in a property. Because you will need a minimum of 10 percent down to buy a property with conventional mortgage financing, we'll limit our search to properties priced under $80,000, so that you can cover the $8,000 down and closing costs.

Searching in the Indianapolis metro area on Owners.com with an $80,000 price limit finds 10 properties. Could any of these qualify as distressed?

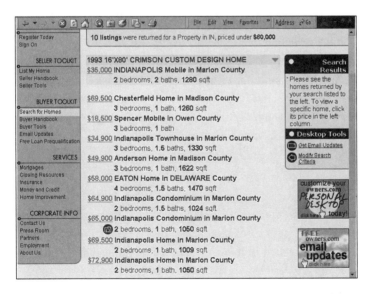

A search on Owners.com for FSBO properties under $80,000 in the metropolitan Indianapolis market turned up 10 properties for consideration as investment opportunities.

Immediately eliminate the mobile homes and the out-of-area properties. Then eliminate the market-priced retail properties (over $60 to $65 per square foot). That leaves us with two possibilities: the 1330 sq. ft. townhouse for $34,900 and the 1622 sq. ft. 3-bedroom, 2-bath home for $49,900 in Anderson (north of Indianapolis).

When I click the links to investigate the two properties further, it turns out that the Anderson property is an old house, built in 1908 with a newer roof (four years old), on a small city lot. It's cheap for the size, but it's old and too far away for a rental. It could possibly be remodeled and sold for a profit, but intuition says this is someone's headache that they would like to get rid of. The townhouse in Indianapolis is quite another story.

According to its description, the townhouse has a motivated seller who can finance the property or sell on a lease-purchase. This 34-year-old townhouse is bargain priced and has been remodeled. There is terrific space for the price. The seller has a second one-bedroom unit in the same complex for $19,900. (These units are cheaper than good used cars.) Why is this owner, who is probably an investor, selling? There must be a crime problem, judging from the comments about security patrols. Is this the reason for the bargain prices, is this just a rundown slum area, or both? The property and location require further research and a drive by to check out the neighborhood. Location is everything, and no one ever said real estate investing was easy.

What this example shows us is that you can go online with sources we've already learned about and find distressed FSBO properties in your own backyard. It's now time for you to try this same exercise in your area. Use the same approach we just used and see what bargains you can find.

Is there a better way to find these distressed investment properties? One investor friend of mine, whose job keeps him on the road, drives through neighborhoods looking for poorly maintained homes with neglected landscaping (high grass and weeds). His assumption—and he has been successful with this technique—is that these types of properties are probably distressed.

Could we go online instead of driving around? There *is* another way, and it's much more efficient.

Classified Ads Online Are the Best Source

Your best sources for finding distressed FSBO properties, in my opinion, are online real estate classified ads from your metropolitan area newspaper or papers. Back in Chapter 4, we covered finding classified ads for FSBO properties. Let's review quickly.

To find any newspaper that has searchable online classified ads, go to this site:

> *http://www.realfind.com*

If this link fails for any reason, use this URL:

> *http://www.bonafideclassified.com*

Both of these addresses take you to a search page from which you choose a state and a city or newspaper name if you know it. The next page lets you choose a newspaper in the area of your interest and work with that paper's online classified system. A quick search of the classifieds, using the keyword *owner*, can bring up some interesting ads from the most recent Sunday real estate classified section. In the sample case I ran on the Indianapolis paper, I note that one ad offers a land contract and another offers a fully leased duplex (or *double*, as these two-family homes are sometimes called). Both are interesting possibilities.

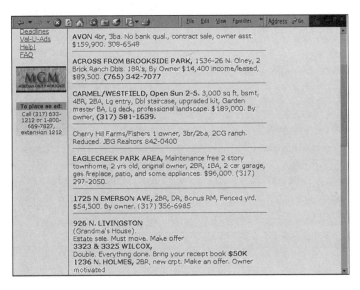

A search of the online classified ads in The Indianapolis Star turned up several interesting investment opportunities.

Sellers do not advertise that they or their properties are distressed. You must infer that definition from the combination of factors and code words used. Some revealing information is given by code words and phrases, such as the following:

Code Words in Ad	What They Really Mean
owner motivated	Could be desperate or just very negotiable
immediate occupancy	Owner moved and is making two mortgage payments, or the property is owned by an investor
owner financing or *contract*	Owner has equity in property, may want the maximum price, or the property will not sell any other way; the property may be substandard or distressed; it may be a "unique" property; the seller may be desperate; the seller may own the property free and clear
price reduced or *priced below appraised value*	The property was overpriced originally and has been on the market too long, or the price is being set for quick sale
owner relocated or *relocating*	The owner is making two mortgage payments now or soon will be
must sell or *bring offers*	Here's a distressed seller or property
handyman special or *fixer-upper*	*Truly* distressed property; proceed with caution
decorating allowance	Internally distressed; needs remodeling or was inhabited by many animals, children, or both
make offer or *must sell by mm/dd/yy*	A distressed seller or property
lease purchase or *rent to buy*	An investor-owned property, with equity
asking $xxx,xxx	Will take substantially less
estate sale	Greedy heirs want to get their cash quickly, rather than get maximum market price

Searching the classifieds with various keywords or keyword combinations, depending on your newspaper's Web site search capabilities, will let you mine the classifieds for real estate gold. Go to *www.realfind.com* now and repeat what we have done here in your metro area newspaper.

Not for Investors Only

If you are not (yet) a real estate investor and are reading this chapter from an owner-occupant's perspective, obviously you can use the techniques described here to find a bargain property for a personal residence. The point to keep in mind is that a bargain for an investor may not be a bargain for you. Investors don't live in the properties they purchase, nor do they live through a renovation.

Investors pick properties rationally for return on investment. There are no emotional factors (or there should not be any) in an investor's decision to buy or not buy a property. Homebuyers, on the other hand, choose a home for many reasons, not all of them rational. In the buying decision, many emotional factors are ultimately more important than any logical fact (as any agent will tell you). Would you buy a below-market-priced fixer-upper in a less desirable neighborhood and school district, live there for several years, and subject your family to a sub-optimum lifestyle (maybe even exposure to drugs and crime) to make $10,000 to $20,000? I wouldn't and I don't think you would either.

If you bargain hunt for your first or next home, make certain that you really want to live in that bargain and its environment. A nightmare scenario is when the distressed bargain property you buy ends up distressing you in the long run.

When sellers get far beyond distressed, they end up in *foreclosure*, which is every homeowner's worst nightmare. Nonetheless, foreclosed properties—whether sold at auction or purchased after foreclosure by the mortgagee—represent opportunities for real estate investors. Using the Internet to find pre-foreclosed properties, foreclosure sales, and repossessed properties is our next topic.

Remember:
Investors buy and rent properties they wouldn't necessarily live in or find desirable themselves. There is always a shortage of affordable single-family rentals. Some renters will always be just that for many reasons (for example, some will be rent subsidy tenants). If demand for rentals is strong, investors can make acceptable rates of return from bargain properties you or I would not want to live in.

Finding Foreclosures and Repos

When a mortgagor defaults on his mortgage note payments, the mortgagee may take the collateral property (the security for the note) through foreclosure. The laws regulating the real estate foreclosure process differ from state to state. Nevertheless, there are some common principles:

At some point, the property will be taken back by the lender, often through a forced sale or foreclosure auction.

There are three opportunities for investors in the foreclosure cycle:

- Pre-foreclosure (while owner is still in possession). You may be able to offer an owner an acceptable alternative to foreclosure, which saves him the agony of the process and allows you to buy well below market price.

- Foreclosure sale or auction. Here you will bid against the mortgagee.

- Bank-owned after foreclosure (repossessed or REO properties). The sooner you can approach the bank after it reacquires the property, the more negotiable the bank will be. If you can get to the mortgagee before it lists the property with a realtor, you will get a better price.

The pre-foreclosure and foreclosure sale information is publicly available at county courthouses across the country. Companies that make a business of collecting and publishing this information from county recorders, online or in print, do so for access or subscription fees. The best of these fee-for-service sites are presented in the next section.

After a mortgage company, the agency (such as Fannie Mae or Freddie Mac), or the bank has acquired a property by foreclosure, it becomes a repo or REO (short for Real Estate Owned). These REO properties can be found easily and without cost by searching the appropriate sites, which we will do in the section "Bank Repo or REO Sites," later in this chapter. To finish our search for bargain properties, we will go to the government sites; the biggies are HUD (for FHA foreclosures) and VA.

Foreclosure Sites

If you are serious about finding foreclosures and want to avoid
weekly trips to various county courthouses, you may want to subscribe to one of the fee-based foreclosure services. My advice is
to request a brief free trial subscription to evaluate the timeliness
and quality of the data provided for your market. A monthly subscription, which you can cancel at any time, is preferable to a
larger up-front annual fee. Here are three of the better subscription sites:

- **Bates Foreclosure Report** (*www.brucebates.com*)

- **ForeclosureNet** (*www.bankhomes.net*)

- **Foreclosures Online** (*www.4close.com*)

Another very useful site with information on foreclosure investing
and many links to listing service sites (particularly for California)
is found here:*www.all-foreclosure.com.*

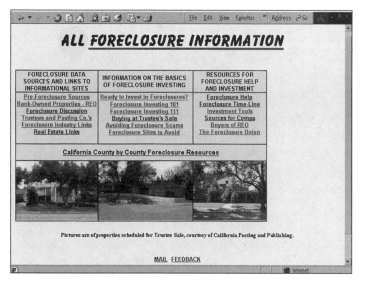

The www.all-fore
closure.com *site
provides some
good information
about foreclosure
investing and
many useful links
to other listing
sites.*

If you are new to real estate investing, you should be aware of the
scams, get-rich-in-real-estate seminar rip-offs, expensive tape
courses, *ad nauseam*, that prey on the inexperienced. This book is
not intended to be a course on real estate investing, but it is about
using the Internet as a resource for investing. To protect yourself

and to get a source of valid real estate investment advice, go to newsletter publisher and author John T. Reed's real estate Web page at this URL:

www.johntreed.com/realestate.html

Check out the "Guru" debunking section and his other information; you will be well served by an authentic expert in the real estate investment field.

After a property has been foreclosed, it becomes a repo or REO (Real Estate Owned) of the lender. The subscription-based sites just listed all contain REO listings. You can find many of these directly (and free) at the sites we review in the next section.

Bank Repo or REO Sites

You may find all the bargains you could ever want at the *free* agency and REO sites. Repossessed properties are usually listed with local real estate companies and will normally be priced closer to retail than wholesale after they enter the bank's portfolio. You can register with the various banks in your state and be notified of new REOs as they become available and before they are listed with realty companies. Banks and mortgage companies are generally more negotiable immediately after the foreclosure auction and before they list the property.

Here are the links and some home pages of the agency sites and some major REO sites. You should always check *www.homesteps.com* if you are looking for a personal residence. This is Freddie Mac's REO site, and it offers special financing (5 percent down with no mortgage insurance) for such properties.

- *www.homesteps.com*

  This is the place for first time homebuyers looking for a bargain property—with special financing included. Don't expect to buy way below market price, but these foreclosed properties have been repaired and put back on the market for quick sale. Investors can buy these properties as well, but without the special financing.

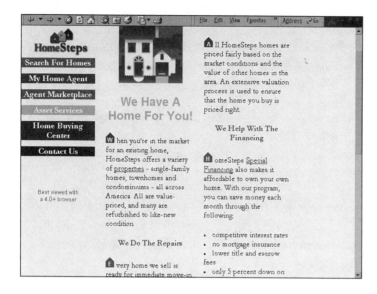

Freddie Mac's REOs are offered through the agency's HomeSteps Web site. If you're not an investor, you can expect some special financing options on the properties offered here.

- *www.fanniemae.com/homes/index.html*

  Check out the REO property listings at Fannie Mae (FNMA) by searching their database. Note that Fannie Mae–owned homes are sold through local real estate brokers. All Fannie Mae–owned homes are listed in the local multiple listing system (MLS); you can access the complete listing by contacting the listing broker.

If these two agency REO property searches don't satisfy you, try these bank REO sites:

- *http://www.premierereo.com/pas_properties.html*

  This site belongs to Premiere Asset Services. They manage REOs for other banks and have a few hundred property listings online with photos. These properties are all listed with local real estate brokers (as is the case with most REOs). After all, what banker is going to go out and show houses?

- *www.bankofamerica.com*

  This is Bank of America's REO site. You won't necessarily find hundreds of listings in every state, but this major national bank's REOs are definitely worth reviewing.

• *http://www.bankreo.com/bankreo/reoframe.htm*

   This is OCWEN Federal Bank's REO site. This bank buys
   nonperforming loans (many of which obviously end up in
   foreclosure) and then manages the foreclosed property resale.

These are only three of many hundreds of potential bank REO
operations. Twenty bucks a month for a subscription to one of the
foreclosure databases is looking better all the time, compared to
searching site by site for REOs in a market area.

Government Repos

There are still more places to go to find REO properties—the
U.S. government has a few thousand foreclosed homes for sale as
the result of defaulted FHA and VA mortgages. Then there are
those drug dealers' houses that the Feds seize....

Visit HUD and VA Online

Buyers Beware:

HUD sells property "as is." If a HUD-foreclosed property has deteriorated to the degree that it is unacceptable for an FHA insured loan, it is sold by HUD as uninsured. You must be *very* careful about the condition of these properties because HUD does not make any pre-sale repairs.

HUD has a vast database of homes for sale. These homes once
had FHA-insured loans, and some but not all are eligible for FHA
loans again. Investors can pick up bargains on HUD homes that
are offered uninsured (which means that the home is no longer
eligible for FHA financing). First-time homebuyers are attracted
to the insured property offerings because HUD, by definition,
allows another FHA loan on the property and often offers incentives to borrowers (such as only $500 or $1,000 down). Buyers
often bid these insured properties up above the offering price
because of the attractive financing.

Investors will want to bid primarily on uninsured properties and
stay away from competing with homeowners. Go to the HUD site
with this direct link and hope it works, or start at *www.hud.gov*
and work your way through this complicated site:

   www.hud.gov/local/sams/ctznhome.html

This link takes you to a state selection page shown in the following figure, from which you can begin your search by state.

hud homes for sale

TOPICS

hud news
audience groups
own a home
rental help
homeless
your community
business
consumer info
complaints
about hud
reading room
handbooks/forms
kids
let's talk
local info
fed one-stops

Check out these listings of HUD homes for sale in your area If you think you want to buy a HUD home, you need to contact a real estate broker in your area who is authorized to sell HUD homes (most are) Your broker will submit your bid for you. Before you begin, you may want to read more about how to buy a HUD Home.

If you are a real estate broker, please read this important information.

Alabama   Kentucky   Ohio
Alaska   Louisiana   Oklahoma
Arizona   Maine   Oregon
Arkansas   Maryland   Pennsylvania
California   Massachusetts   Puerto Rico/US
  • Northern   Michigan   Virgin Islands
  • Southern   Minnesota   Rhode Island
Colorado   Mississippi   South Carolina
Connecticut   Missouri   South Dakota
Delaware   Montana   Tennessee
District of   Nebraska   Texas
Columbia   Nevada   Utah
Florida   • Northern   Vermont
Georgia   • Central/Southern Virginia
Hawaii   New Hampshire   Washington
Idaho   New Jersey   West Virginia
Illinois   New Mexico   Wisconsin
Indiana   New York   Wyoming
Iowa   North Carolina
Kansas   North Dakota

HUD's huge selection of homes for sale should be searched, starting here, by both homebuyers and investors.

Through its loan guarantee program, the Veterans Administration (VA) insures lenders for mortgage loans made to veterans. When these loans default (which happens much more rarely than it does for FHA loans), the VA offers the foreclosed homes for sale. The bargain properties may be few, but you should search the site at *www.vba.va.gov/bln/loan/homes.htm* to see what properties are offered in your market.

GSA Auctions

To round out the possibilities of finding bargain investment property, let's conclude this chapter with a look at the GSA (General Services Administration) property auctions. If you need a lighthouse or a missile silo, you might find it here:

http://propertydisposal.gsa.gov/property/

Treasury Department Seizures

To get a deal on a drug dealer's house seized by the Feds, check out this site:

www.treas.gov/auctions/customs

If the houses don't suit your tastes, try the boats. They get some nice ones down in Miami.

GSA auctions are the place to find unusual investment opportunities, such as a surplus naval base.

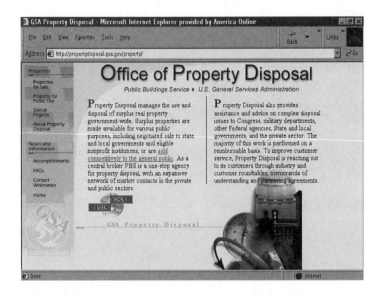

Wrapping It Up

After diligently studying this chapter, you should have learned

- How and where to search for distressed FSBO properties

- Where to go online to find foreclosures

- Some sources for finding bank-owned and agency-owned properties

- What the government has to offer for investors, including where to find a nice missile silo to rehab

The intent of this chapter was *not* to teach "Real Estate Investing 101" but to show you how to use the Internet to find bargain properties, either distressed or foreclosed. These properties are the targets of experienced real estate investors. You now have an arsenal of online weapons at your disposal to become a killer real estate investor.

CHAPTER 10

Financing Investment Property

Mortgage Considerations for Investors

How you finance investment property depends on the investment objective you planned to achieve when making the purchase. In this chapter, we will discuss two different financing approaches and how to use the Internet to help find appropriate lenders, depending on the approach taken.

Often, an investor will need to minimize down payment and closing costs to conserve capital for needed rehabilitation. Sometimes a larger investment in the property is required or appropriate. First, we will consider two different investment objectives and their effect on financing choices. Later, we will go online to find some investor-friendly lenders and some lenders of last resort, the so-called "hard money" lenders.

Buy and Hold

You've found a large, older brick duplex in a quiet neighborhood, and the price from the motivated, retired owner is reasonable because he's ready to quit being a landlord. Both units are currently leased, the rents total $1,350 per month, and taxes are only $1,200 per year. Both units need interior paint, and the landscaping is beyond ugly, but there are no other major defects. The owner has accepted your offer of $100,000 but will not carry any owner financing. He wants cash. You have up to $20,000 you can invest. What should you do about financing this nearly ideal rental property?

What You'll Learn in This Chapter:

▶ The mortgage financing considerations for buy-and-hold versus quick-turn investments

▶ How to find online lenders to fund investment real estate

▶ What *hard money* loans are and where to find them

▶ Where to find the truth about those "no money down" real estate infomercials on late-night cable TV

Your objective for this property is to *buy and hold* for income and appreciation. You follow the old but still useful 10-10-10 real estate investing rule:

- Buy at 10 percent or more under the market

- Pay no more than 10 percent interest

- Invest 10 percent or less as a cash down payment

You want to find a lender who will lend 90 percent on investment property, and you want the lowest rate with the lowest costs you can find. You are willing to pay discount points to permanently buy down the rate because you are planning to hold this property indefinitely.

Here are some basic guidelines for mortgage-financed, buy-and-hold income property:

- Depending on your investment rate of return requirements and your investment capital available, make down payments of 10 to 30 percent.

- Buy the interest rate down to an APR in the 7.5–8.5 percent range, if possible.

- Amortize for 15 years if you want to take cash out of the property by refinancing later, or for 30 years to maximize cash flow from rental income.

- Debt service (your mortgage and escrow payment) ideally should not exceed 75 percent of gross rental income. Combined with reasonable maintenance costs and low vacancy, this will produce excellent cash flow.

When you buy and hold rental property, you are sensitive to interest rates and cash flow. This is just common sense. It means that you want the lowest cost of ownership so that the market rental rate gives you positive cash flow for an acceptable rate of return on your investment. What about speculative buying for resale? Are the financing considerations different?

Quick Turn

The real estate investment gurus—those guys in the infomercials—would have you believe you can turn nothing into millions. *Nothing* means that you have no money to invest, no experience, and no training in real estate. Yet these smiling salesmen of tapes, books, seminars, and "boot camps" are going to transform you into Donald Trump overnight.

Not likely. When you see those infomercials, you should ask yourself, "Why are they selling $69 tape courses on TV when they could be making millions in real estate?" The answer, of course, is that mass direct marketing of information using television infomercials is vastly more profitable, more quickly, than real estate investing.

Real estate investing is hard work. Although the profits *can* be spectacular, for the novice there are no legal, easy, get-rich-quick schemes that work.

There *is*, however, a legitimate speculative real estate investment technique. I call it *quick turn*. Other experts call it *flipping* or *quick flip* or something similar. The idea is to buy distressed property requiring minimal rehab and then sell it as a FSBO as quickly as possible. This is like the business concept of inventory turns: The more times you turn (sell) your inventory per year, the higher your annualized rate of return on your invested capital.

Debunking the Experts:
For an eye-opening debunking of these so-called "experts," read John T. Reed's information at *www.johntreed.com/realestate.html*.

For example, if you have $10,000 to invest and can buy and sell four houses per year at a net profit of $5,000 each, your $10,000 turns over four times per year, generating $5,000 each time for a total return of $20,000. This is an annualized rate of return of more than 200 percent. The next year, you have $30,000 to invest, either in higher-priced properties or in more low-priced properties.

Is this realistic? Four houses bought and sold in a year is aggressive for a part-time investor, but it could be done with luck and a lot of effort. Can the average investor make $5,000 net profit per transaction? If you buy and sell without paying a real estate agent's commission, buy the property at the right price, and properly control rehab expenses (this usually means doing it yourself), the answer is *yes*. Is this a lot of hard work? Again, the answer is *yes*.

What are the mortgage financing implications of speculative real estate purchases?

- Since the holding period is short, you don't care as much about interest rates. What you want to do is minimize the cost of the transaction. You should pay no points or origination fees.

- Trade a higher rate for lower loan-closing costs. It is possible that you will make only one or two mortgage payments before the property sells.

- You want to invest the smallest possible down payment.

We are looking for a 90 percent (or even 95 percent) mortgage, low closing costs, a rate not to exceed 10 percent, and a lender that can close quickly. Is this difficult? Yes it is. Is it impossible? No, it is done all the time.

In the spring of 1998, my wife and I, with a partner, did exactly the type of transaction just described. We accepted a higher interest rate on the loan to minimize closing costs, invested only 10 percent in the down payment, and spent less than $2,000 on rehab, mostly for interior and exterior painting. The details of that transaction are summarized in Table 10.1.

Table 10.1   Quick Turn Purchase and Sale of a Single-Family Residence

A.	Purchase Price 3/24/98	$103,000	What we paid the distressed seller
B.	Net Cost	$105,145	Includes closing costs
C.	Mortgage	$(92,700)	10% down, 30 years @ 9.75%
D.	Cash Invested	$12,445	B–C; $6,222 from each partner
E.	Sale Price 7/8/98	$119,500	FSBO; no commission paid
F.	Gross Profit	$14,335	E–B; before closing costs
G.	Rents Received	$2,390	Seller lease-back for 2 months @ $1,195 per month
H.	Rehab, Carrying, Selling, and Closing Costs	($6,469)	Includes 3 months of mortgage payments at $984 per month
I.	Net Pre-tax	$10,256	F + G–H; $5,128 Profit in cash to each partner

As you can see from the accounting for this transaction, each partner invested $6,222 in cash (plus countless hours in painting, cleaning, and showing the property); in 3.5 months, each partner made a cash profit of $5,128. Annualized, this is a 282 percent rate of return on invested capital (not counting the obvious value of the partners' labor).

Clearly though, this was no get-rich-quick scheme. It was risky as well. If the property had lingered on the market another few months, or if it had become necessary to pay a 7 percent agent's commission, our profit could have totally evaporated. Real estate quick turn investing is not for the lazy or faint of heart.

Now it is time to go online and find some appropriate lenders to help us invest, whatever our investment objective.

Investor-Friendly Online Lenders

There is a basic dilemma for real estate investors who want to use the Internet to compare rates and loan programs. Most online direct national lenders and those soliciting for their markets are not interested in investor loans or will not originate them online. Some of the reasons for this are

- Investor loans are more difficult to originate, because investors tend to have complex financial situations.

- The loans are *full documentation*, which are slower to process and approve.

- They are usually smaller loans than owner-occupied pur-chase-money mortgages.

- Investors have less commitment to the transaction than an owner-occupant does.

For these and other reasons relating to secondary market issues, online lenders do not seek out the business of investors. This is also true of local mortgage companies. Loan officers like to do easy, conventional purchase-money mortgages for single-family personal residences. They make more money faster with these loans—especially with higher loan amounts—than they do with investor loans.

Lessons Learned:
When it comes to quick turn investing, remember the old cliché: "No guts, no glory." On the other hand, the partners in this example were so burned out from the effort required for this transaction, on top of their full-time jobs, that they did not make another real estate invest-ment that year.

Ask any loan officer if he would rather do a $180,000 conventional loan for a corporate relocation buyer or a $60,000 investor loan for a local part-time real estate investor who wants to buy and rehab a duplex. Because of the extra work and hassle, only one in 50 will prefer the investor loan, although it might be possible to make more commission on an investor loan.

Online lenders are in a high-volume, commodity business, and investor loans don't fit that mold. What's an investor to do? We'll have to do some sleuthing to find national and local sources for investor loans from online lenders.

Finding the Best National Lenders

FYI:
LTV stands for *loan-to-value*. It is the ratio of loan amount to purchase price. For example, an $80,000 loan on a $100,000 property has an 80 percent LTV.

If we go back to some of the online lenders we learned about in Chapter 7, "Financing Your Dream Home," we discover some interesting facts. For example, if you wanted to borrow $90,000 on the purchase of a $100,000 duplex, here is what you would find with some of the big name online lenders:

Mortgage.com	70% LTV on 2-4 unit property
Interloan.com	70% LTV on 2-4 unit property
Loansurfer.com	80% LTV, 1-unit single-family only

This is not very encouraging, because we would like to invest 10 percent or less. There are 95-percent investor loans available in the market, but very few lenders offer them, and none of the online lenders offer them.

Investor loans at 90 percent LTV are more common; fortunately, we can find them at our popular online lenders. Both iOwn.com (*www.iown.com*) and E-LOAN (*www.eloan.com*) offer 90 percent LTV investor loans, and we can search them for rates.

To search iOwn.com, from the home page, select your state under Shop Rates and hit Search. You must then modify the Loan and Property Assumptions form by scrolling down on the resulting RateShopper page.

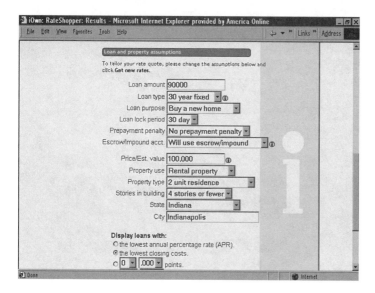

iOwn.com's Loan and Property Assumptions form must be modified when you are searching for rates for investor loans.

Here is how you should fill out the form. First, you specify the desired loan amount at exactly 90 percent of the purchase price. (Note that an LTV greater than 90 percent will be rejected.) If you are planning to resell the property within three to five years, specify No Prepayment Penalty. If you plan to hold the property indefinitely, then you don't care about the prepayment penalty and you can increase the number of loan choices or improve your rate. An escrow/impound account will normally be required, so leave the default choice in place. In the property description fields, specify the price, select Rental Property for Property Use, and complete the rest of the form as appropriate.

If you want a quick turn investment loan, you can select the Lowest Closing Cost option under the Display Loans With: heading. The assumption here is that the property will be resold quickly and that lower costs are more significant than interest rate over the holding period.

When the sample form is submitted, the search results present only one lender's program and rate as seen in the following figure, illustrating the point that there are fewer loan options available to investors.

Results of rate search for 90 percent LTV investor loan from iOwn.com. Only one lender was found for this type of loan.

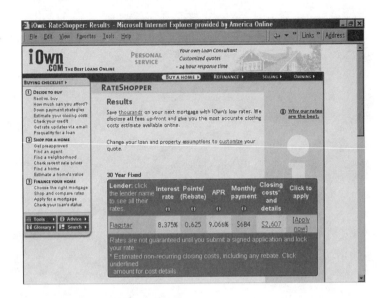

Additional Investor Site:

Another lender that offers investor and commercial loans and lends nationwide is American Mutual Mortgage, LLC, of Atlanta, Georgia (*www.amer icanmutual.com*).

If we use exactly the same search parameters and go to E-LOAN (*www.eloan.com*), we get two loan choices. When I performed this search, the E-LOAN rates and APRs were significantly higher than the iOwn.com rates, emphasizing the need to do careful rate comparison shopping for these less commonly offered investor loans.

What we need is a quick way to find local lenders that we can query for rates and programs. This is especially important if there are special financial circumstances, such as a need for low- or no-documentation features or programs to accommodate impaired credit.

Find a Local Lender Online if You Can

How can we find a local lender? Obviously, we could spend hours with the Yellow Pages and the telephone, trying to find a lender who will (a) call us back and (b) show even the slightest interest (no pun intended) in our investor loan requirements. Alternatively, we could go online and give the Net a shot at finding a suitable local lender.

Some of the sites you have seen earlier in this book can help us again. You may recall from Chapter 7 that LendingTree (*www.lendingtree.com*) will provide lender quotes on your specific loan program requests after you input a complete loan application. This is an excellent service, but probably should be done *after* you screen some other lenders and determine whether your deal is fundable or out in left field, with a very low probability of approval. Loans in this category would have one or more factors such as high LTV, no income verification, or impaired credit.

To get a list of lenders in your market who offer loans with specific features, query Interest.com, using this link:

www.mortgagerates.com/features/index.html

You go directly to a search form, where you enter your state and then choose from a drop-down list of loan programs. The problem with this directory search of lenders is that it is not very refined. It seems to produce about the same list of lenders for each different loan program. In fact, some of the results are erroneous. Use this search to identify a list of possible sources and then link directly to the lenders' Web sites to verify their offerings. This approach is faster than calling from the Yellow Pages.

Another approach to finding a lender for your particular investor loan is one mentioned at the end of Chapter 7. You can get lenders to contact you, based on your loan profile, by using Computer Loan Network's auction-like services at *www.clnet.com*. Enter your profile of requirements, and lenders who subscribe to the CLN service will contact you if they are interested in your loan. This approach puts the ball in the lender's court, so to speak, and you will hear from only those lenders that can actually provide what you need.

Look for a Better Deal:

If you already have a rate quote, you can use the CLN service to find lenders that will possibly quote you a better rate.

Another excellent approach to finding the right lender for your investor loan is by referral from other real estate investors. If your city has a real estate investors' (REI) club or association (sometimes called *landlord associations*), you should join and network with other investors.

To quickly find an REI club, go to *www.creonline.com* to reach the home page of Creative Real Estate Online. This site has links to REI clubs in most states. It will save you time and effort trying to figure out whether your local club has a listed telephone number.

Additional information resources on the CRE Online site are worth your perusal. Check out the list of information, interaction, and inspiration links on the left side of the page. You will have to scroll down the home page to reach the link to the REI query page, where you select your state to see the listing of clubs.

Creative Real Estate Online has links to real estate investment (REI) clubs in most states plus much more information for investors and investor wannabes.

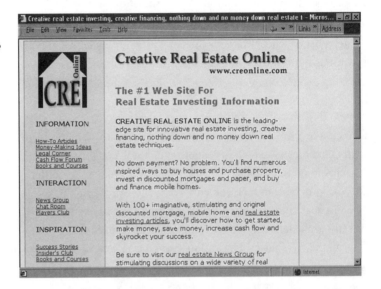

What do you do if none of the resources covered so far can satisfy your unique investor financing needs? You may have to go after some "hard money," which is our next topic.

Hard Money Lenders

If you can tolerate the costs and rates, there are lenders that can lend you cash quickly to buy and renovate that bargain property you just found. These lenders, euphemistically called *hard money lenders*, can be extremely helpful under the right circumstances.

Hard money refers to asset-based lending. The collateral property is the primary consideration, with the income and credit-worthiness of the borrower of secondary importance. Consequently, risk is managed by offering low loan-to-value (LTV) ratios, charging high rates and points, and offering short terms. The *hard* in *hard money* also refers to the costs and terms.

Know What You Are Getting Into

Your hard money lender may offer you a loan that seems attractive for your objectives, but you should know what you are getting into. For example, you may find a property for $75,000 in need of major renovation that would appraise for $120,000 after the repairs are completed. Because you have blemished credit and are currently unemployed, no normal bank mortgage lender will even return your calls, although you own six rental houses and have $40,000 in your checking account. Still, you *might* find a hard money deal with these parameters:

- 50 percent LTV against the appraised value ($60,000 loan amount)

- 16 percent interest, 1 year balloon, monthly interest only

- 6 points cost ($4,680)

Note that you'd need at least $20,000 to close on the property, plus your rehab funds (maybe another $20,000), but the lender does not require income verification. Credit is not an issue as long as you are not in bankruptcy and can verify sufficient funds for closing and rehab costs. Do you see where the term "hard money" gets its name?

Another hard money lender might lend 80 percent of your purchase price (on the same $60,000 loan) and 80 percent of your renovation costs (another $16,000), which could be attractive for our example. Because your down payment would be $15,000 in this example and you could borrow 80 percent of the estimated $20,000 renovation costs, your total cash outlay would be $19,000 plus points and closing costs. Your total cash requirement in this example would be at least $16,000 less than in the first case.

Where can you go to find these friendly hard money lenders? Hmm, maybe the Internet?

Hard Money Private and Portfolio Lenders

Most hard money and portfolio lenders fall into the commercial lending arena and will not originate small (under $500,000) loans.

For the individual real estate investor, these commercial lenders
are inappropriate, unless you are trying to finance an apartment
complex. However, there are some exceptions. First, we will look
at two national portfolio/hard money sources: One does smaller
loans, and the other does only large loans. To finish up, we'll look
at two other ways of finding commercial lenders online.

Point your browser now to *www.galaresources.com* and go to the
home page of Gala Resources, a nationwide hard money and private portfolio lender that has a minimum loan limit of $50,000.
They do not offer an online application service, which you will
find is typical of commercial lenders. Each loan these specialized
lenders do is unique and requires a significant documentation
review to determine feasibility. By definition, these kinds of
investor loans are not cookie cutter, conforming loans that can be
computer submitted and underwritten.

*New York–based
Gala Resources
has flexible
investor hard
money loans start-
ing at $50,000.*

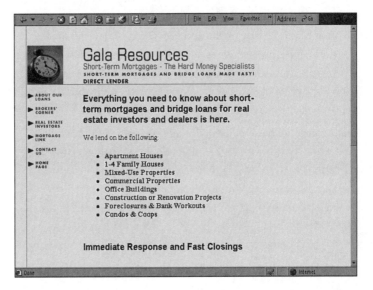

If your goal is to buy a 100-unit apartment complex that's on the
market for a paltry $1.5 million, you may want to contact a com-
mercial lender such as Guardian Mortgage. Go to Guardian's
home page at *www.guardianmortgage.com* and click the Recent
Transactions link to see the type of loans they make. Let's hope
your real estate investing is so successful that you'll need their
services, because their minimum loan amount is $750,000.

Portfolio lender Guardian Mortgage does large commercial loans with a minimum loan amount of $750,000.

To finish our search for specialized lenders, let's turn to two different directory sites. Go now to *www.blackburne.com* to reach the 1ˢᵗ AAA Commercial Mortgage Lender Databank, a service provided by Blackburne & Brown Mortgage Company, Inc., a California commercial mortgage banker.

From the Commercial Mortgage Search link, you can enter your loan parameters to search a database of 750 lenders for lenders and rates for your specific situation. This is an interesting and informative site to explore to learn more about specialized commercial lending.

The final site we'll use in searching for portfolio and other special-situation commercial loans is the National Financial Services Network (*www.nfsn.com*). This directory site has listings by state and type of loan. After selecting a state, you choose a type of financial service category. A list of lenders within that category is then presented. You can find sources for everything from apartment loans to aircraft leases to venture capital. Need some seed capital for your pre-IPO, dot-com company? Find it here while you look for financing for your corporate headquarters.

Wrapping It Up

In this chapter, we have briskly studied, and learned a few important things about, financing investment property:

- The different mortgage parameters to consider for buy-and-hold versus quick-turn investments.

- How to find national and local online lenders to fund investment real estate loans.

- What *hard money* loans are and where to find them.

As a bonus, we learned that making money in real estate is hard but financially rewarding. Perhaps the most valuable bonus was a Web site that debunks the "no-money-down, get rich quick in real estate" gurus you've seen on late-night cable TV infomercials. If creating wealth were as easy as these charlatans claim, we would all be filthy rich.

Now that we've learned some lessons about financing investment real estate with help from the Internet, let's move on to learn how to *sell* that bargain handyman special you bought and just renovated. We'll use the Net to help sell that beauty fast—*before* your hard money balloon note is due.

CHAPTER 11

Use the Net to Market Investment Property

Now that you own investment property, this chapter teaches you some additional online marketing techniques you can use to help sell your property. Most of what you have already learned about selling real estate using the Internet obviously applies when you are an investor selling one of your portfolio properties. However, there are differences between investor and owner-occupant sellers that shape the marketing strategies used.

The FSBO homeowner, who is perhaps simply trading up in the same market, can spend months marketing his home and hold out for the top market price. As an investor with scarce capital now tied up in your property, you have to sell quickly—especially if your carrying costs are not covered by rental income. In addition, you are not about to give up 7 percent of your sale price and hard-earned profit to real estate agents.

Although much of what you already learned in Chapter 5, "Sell Your Home Yourself and Save Thousands," is applicable, this chapter focuses on using some additional techniques (both marketing and financial) to sell your investment property. We will take advantage of every Internet resource we can find to help us sell quickly at maximum profit.

Notice that, as investors, we want to maximize profit. *This does not necessarily imply maximizing our selling price.* We must always look at trade-offs between profit and selling price. All investments have carrying costs and opportunity costs. In real estate investing, when you are ready to sell, you want to move your capital into another investment, real estate or otherwise.

The longer it takes to sell an investment:

1. The greater the carrying costs.

2. The opportunity cost rises.

3. The yield on your invested capital decreases.

Items 1 and 3 are fairly obvious. Number 2 warrants some discussion. *Opportunity cost* refers to the lost income or investment return from opportunities foregone or delayed because of the current investment or investment choice. If you have $20,000 tied up in a vacant rental property that is on the market, that $20,000 is not available for other investment opportunities. At a minimum, your opportunity cost is the yield you could obtain on a totally safe investment in U.S. Treasury bills. The serious opportunity costs come from being unable to make another timely investment or missing out completely on an opportunity.

Let's say that a very attractive, bargain-priced property comes on the market and you want to buy it, as do other investors and homebuyers. You have had one of your own properties on the market for months. You have been holding out for top dollar and have rejected several offers that were three to five thousand below your asking price. The property you now want to buy has a potential profit of $15,000 after renovation. It sells to another investor for $2,500 less than you would have offered for the property. You could have been the successful buyer, but your money was tied up in your current property. What was your "opportunity cost" of holding out for a maximum sales price for your own property? Your cost was the $15,000 profit lost by not buying the new property, less the difference between your asking price and the best offer made on your property. In this example, your opportunity cost was at least $12,000. Real estate is an illiquid investment. It takes time to sell—and time is of the essence in investing.

Online marketing can help shorten the selling cycle for investment property. Let's see how.

Online Marketing for Investors

Now let's look at some of the ways the online marketing of investment property differs from the marketing of owner-occupied property. There are many similarities in marketing both types, of

course, but investors have special circumstances that affect the
approach.

Selling to First-Time Homebuyers

One of the advantages you have as an investor is flexibility in
selling your property to first-time homebuyers. You should have
equity in your investment property of at least 15 percent or more
(probably 20 to 30 percent), whereas most homeowners have 10
percent or less net equity (after selling costs). You can offer concessions and incentives that other owner-occupant sellers cannot
afford to offer. Because the number one obstacle to home ownership for first-time buyers is funds to close, you can help by paying closing costs or by offering some seller financing (or down
payment assistance, as we will learn).

Remember:
If you bought your investment property at least 10 percent below market, put down 5 to 10 percent, and enhanced the value through some remodeling, you should have 20 percent or more equity in the property when you sell.

The argument that you don't need to offer concessions to first-
time homebuyers doesn't wash. If your property was a former
rental home and is priced just below or at the average home price
for homes its size in your area, only two types of buyers will be
interested. First will be other investors hoping to beat your price
down and pick up a rental property with a successful history.
Second will be first-time homebuyers. Other investors are not
going to pay retail for your property; therefore, you will have to
discount the price to sell to investors. And it is unlikely that a current homeowner will be trading up to buy your rental property
(the most common reason existing homeowners buy). More than
likely, your best prospect will be a former tenant in your property.
Builders and tract home developers target first-time homebuyers
and offer substantial incentives and concessions because they
know these former renters have low cash savings. You are competing with them and every other seller of an existing home in
your price range. First-time homebuyers are your target market;
more often than not, you will have to help them buy your property.

You want to sell quickly and maximize your profit. The first-time
homebuyer is interested in two issues: the monthly payment and
how much cash is required to buy the property. They are not as
concerned about price as they are about being able to afford the
payments and the down payment. The basic strategy is to sell at

full market value but to offer concessions that lower the buyer's cash requirements.

Let's get into the details of two techniques to help buyers buy your investment property with your cooperation. The first involves 100 percent financing and down payment assistance; the second concerns owner financing and note selling.

Offer 100 Percent Financing

One of the best ways to entice first-time buyers to your property is to offer 100 percent financing for their home purchase. You can find local lenders in your market area who offer 100 percent LTV programs—either true 100 percent purchase money first mortgages or 80/20 programs in which you (or they) provide the required 20 percent second mortgage. The problem with the 100 percent programs is that they will be subprime loans at a higher interest rate, loans that perhaps make it more difficult for your buyer to qualify. You can help by paying points and closing costs. By paying discount points, you can buy down the rate for your buyer. If you are selling an $80,000 property in which your profit margin is $10,000, you can afford to pay the buyer's loan closing costs, including a point or two if needed to make the deal work.

You need to establish a close working relationship with a competent loan officer at a mortgage company that offers a full spectrum of loan products, from conventional to governments and subprime. If you want to try working with an online lender that lends nationwide, check out this site:

www.quikmortgage.com

QuikMortgage is a division of Greater Atlantic Mortgage Corporation and lends in all 50 states (with some exceptions on some products). You may find that referring your buyers to a local lender with whom you have a relationship is easier than working with an online lender, but online origination, even for difficult loans, is the future of mortgage lending.

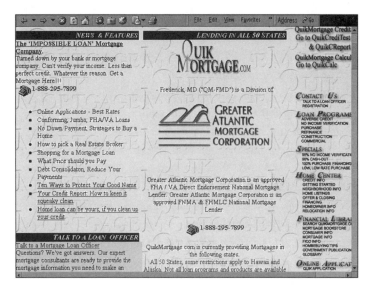

QuikMortgage.com offers 100 percent LTV loan programs nationwide.

Offer Down Payment Assistance

The only *legal* way (in my experience) for a seller to fund the borrower's down payment in the context of traditional mortgage lending is through an FHA loan with a gift from the Nehemiah Program. Refer to Chapter 2, "For First-Time Homebuyers Only," for the details of this program, or go online to this site:

www.nehemiahprogram.com

From the home page, click the Real Estate Professionals link and download the program materials. You will have to find a local lender who participates in the program. Starting at the home page again, click the Homebuyers link and enter your zip code to see if lenders are listed for your area.

The Nehemiah Program, which may be disallowed under a proposed HUD rule revision, gives an FHA buyer the required 3 percent down payment as a gift, provided that the seller remits a 4 percent service fee to the Nehemiah non-profit organization at closing. Over 23,000 home purchases have been assisted with these down payment gifts to date. HUD has acquiesced so far in this apparent circumvention of FHA guidelines on seller concessions. (FHA guidelines, like all conventional lending guidelines, do not permit the seller to contribute any part of the buyer's down payment.) Check back frequently to the Nehemiah Web site to determine whether you will be able to take advantage of this exceptional program.

Offer Owner Financing

One of the advantages you may have as an investor selling your own property is that, with sufficient equity, you can offer some owner financing to facilitate the sale to a first-time homebuyer. For example, assume that you paid $60,000 for a fixer-upper with $6,000 down and a $54,000 first mortgage. Your improvements created a lovely home in first-class condition, which you rented for three years. A fee appraiser has appraised the property conservatively at $90,000. You are ready to sell, having recovered your renovation costs from a strong $300 per month positive cash flow from rent. Your cost basis in the property for tax purposes is just over $70,000.

Your actual cash investment at this point is just $6,000; your mortgage payoff is about $52,700. Your buyer can only qualify for a 75 percent first mortgage ($67,500) from a subprime lender because of a bankruptcy less than two years ago. The lender will allow a seller-financed second mortgage of 20 percent of the purchase price and requires the buyer to have 5 percent of his or her own funds for a down payment. This arrangement is called a 75/20/5.

You had attracted your buyer by advertising owner financing, and now you are ready to structure the deal. Because your objective is not to hold this paper for income, you set the terms to favor selling the note at a later date or at the closing table. You agree to finance $18,000 (the 20 percent) with a second mortgage at 11 percent with a 15-year amortization and a 5-year balloon. Your note broker (see the next section) has agreed to buy your note at the closing table for $13,500 or, after 12 months of satisfactory payments, for $14,200. You decide to take the money at closing because you have another property in mind to buy. Table 11.1 shows how the seller-financed deal compares to other possible deals: an FHA/Nehemiah and an FHA with seller-paid costs.

Table 11.1 Sample Sale with Owner Financing Compared with Two Types of FHA Sales

	75/20/5 Full Price Sale	FHA/Nehemiah with 4% Service Fee	FHA with Seller-Paid Costs of 3%
Sale Price	$90,000	$90,000	$90,000
Cash from Buyer's DP	$4,500	$2,700	$2,700
Cash from 1st Mortgage	$67,500	$87,300	$87,300
Total Cash	$71,500	$90,000	$90,000
Payoff (Seller's Mortgage)	($52,700)	($52,700)	($52,700)
Seller Paid Closing Costs	($450)	($950)	($3,150)
Other Fees	N/A	($3,600)	N/A
Note Sale	$13,500	N/A	N/A
Net to Seller	$31,850	$32,750	$34,150

You would net more from a sale to a qualified FHA buyer in this example, but if owner financing produced a faster sale, this could be your best option. There are other ways to analyze this transaction, and holding the second mortgage for some period is clearly an option to consider. Most investors like cash on hand to pursue the next deal.

How can we use the Internet to find buyers for our owner-financed mortgages?

Sell Your Paper for Cash

If you offer seller-financed first or second mortgages or sell on land contracts, who can you get to buy your paper and how do you find them? The so-called *cash flow industry* is thriving on the Internet. You can find note buyers and brokers who will purchase your paper and sites where you can list your note for sale to note buyers.

Because of the time value of money, you will be selling your note at a discount to its remaining face value. Because your stream of payments extends far into the future, to get a lump sum today for your future payments, a note buyer will calculate a discounted value for your note to satisfy his investment yield. The quality of

FYI:

When you help finance the sale of a property you own, you take a note from the buyer in lieu of cash for part of the selling price. This note is usually secured by a second mortgage or deed of trust. Sometimes called "taking back a second," the note, or *paper*, you hold can often be sold to a note investor at a discount, for cash.

your note, the length of seasoning, the term, the interest rate, the balloon payoff date (if any), and the type of property collateral are all factors that figure into the note buyer's evaluation and calculations. You will want to shop your note to several potential buyers to get the best deal.

On the Internet, you can find note buyers and learn about the note-buying industry, or the diversified cash flow industry, as it is sometimes called. To get a basic understanding of note buying and selling, go to these two excellent sites and spend some time with each:

> www.noteworthyusa.com
> www.papersourceonline.com

The NoteWorthy Web site is both informational and a portal for access to the note buying and selling industry. The Paper Source site publishes a highly regarded newsletter covering the entire cash flow industry. You will find both of these sites—and their links to sources—very helpful.

The Paper Source publishes a highly-regarded newsletter covering the entire cash flow industry. Learn about selling notes here.

After you have a general understanding of the cash flow industry, you may want to explore some additional sites where you can list your note for sale or deal directly with individual note buyers.

- **America's Note Network** (*http://notenetwork.com*) is an example of a site that accepts free note listings from prospective note sellers.

- **Boston Note** (*www.bostonnote.com*) is a direct purchaser of notes that will quote your note purchase after you submit an online quote form.

There are many other note brokers and buyers on the Internet. Search with any search engine using *note buyer* or *trust deeds* or *structured settlements* as your search string, and you will find hundreds of sites. In addition to the two excellent sites just listed, you may want to check these:

- *www.chasefinancial.org* (buyers)

- *www.nationalcontractbuyers.com* (buyers)

- *www.realestatenotes.com* (buyers)

- *www.notefinders.com* (note listings)

If you are, or intend to be, a serious real estate investor, you owe it to yourself (really, no pun intended) to explore the note industry.

Promoting Prime Properties to Owner Occupants

If your investment property is more upscale than a first-time homebuyer would consider, you might have a *prime property* to market. You differ from other owner-occupant sellers of similar properties because you probably have more equity than they do and can offer some incentives to buyers to make your property more attractive. An offer bundled with special financing (using your favorite loan officer) can attract buyers and differentiate your property in the market.

Because you will be an FSBO, but without the possible greed or ego of a homeowner, you can structure a permanent or temporary buydown for the buyer's mortgage, if the buyer works with your preferred lender. Likewise, you can be more open to real estate agents who have qualified buyers and can agree to pay a 3 or 3.5

percent buyer's agent commission. There is one hard-and-fast rule for selling prime properties:

You Must Be a FSBO

If you studied Chapter 5, you are well aware of the FSBO listing sites and online marketing resources available to you. You are bold enough to be a real estate investor, so don't be shy when it comes to maximizing your profits. You can sell your own property and retain the 6 or 7 percent commission a less-adept seller would have to pay a realty agent. You must have a customer focus and be willing to work with buyers at their convenience. It is time consuming to show your property to buyers, but then it's time consuming to make six or seven thousand dollars at whatever you do for a living. Don't leave money on the table when you have worked hard and shrewdly to buy, improve, and then sell an investment property. Be a FSBO! You can do it!

Online Marketing Essentials for Investors

Here are a few guidelines for you to consider when you go online to market your investment property:

- Take the time to get excellent digital photography of your property, inside and out.

- Use every free FSBO site that offers one or more pictures per listing.

- Use several of the paid FSBO sites that allow multiple photos per listing.

- Make certain that you use the Owners.com site.

- Contact *www.ipix.com* about their package deal for a virtual tour.

- Create (or have created for you) a simple Web site to feature your property (with a virtual tour) and reference the home page in every FSBO listing and every classified ad.

- Be willing to show your property on demand, especially to out-of-state buyers who are in town briefly and are working with an agent.

- Promote your listing by email to agents (if you are willing to pay some amount of commission) and indicate that you are an investor and a highly motivated seller, and that the property has immediate occupancy (if it does).

- Offer incentives as appropriate to attract buyers or to close the sale.

- Remember opportunity cost and your carrying costs and the need to reinvest your capital sooner rather than later. Be negotiable if price is the issue. Never let a $1,000 to $2,500 price difference lose a sale.

Quick-Turn Techniques Using the Net

Your need to sell your investment quickly may sometimes outweigh all other considerations. You may need a quick turn transaction for any number of reasons. Typically, if you have renovated a fixer-upper and it took longer or cost more than planned, your carrying costs and over-budget expense may require a very quick sale. If you have a prime rental property (now that you've rehabbed it), you may be able to flip your property to another investor who buys and holds it for the rental income. You will have to price the property and offer terms (perhaps owner financing of some amount) that will be attractive to another investor.

Remember that all knowledgeable investors attempt to buy at substantial discounts from the current market value. Even the buy-and-hold rental property investor will want a deal on a pristine, freshly rehabbed property. They know that if you are approaching them, you have a problem. If you have to cut your losses or sell before you start having losses, opt for the quick, break-even (if possible) sale to another investor.

The best way to find investors who will move quickly and help (read *take advantage of*) you with your problem property is through your local real estate investor club or landlord association. See the discussion in Chapter 9, "How to Find Bargain Properties Online," and revisit Creative Real Estate Online (*www.creonline.com*) to find a local real estate investor club, if you are not already a member in your area.

If you need to move fast and want to consider an auction, read on.

How to Auction Investment Property Online

You can sell anything at auction on the Internet, even real estate. Although real estate auction sites are in their infancy, at some point the eBay of real estate auction sites will emerge. For now, we attempt to sell investment property at auction in several ways, none of which is optimum, but this is a rapidly growing area of e-commerce, so stay tuned.

Real estate has been sold on eBay; current auctions can be found under the Miscellaneous category, an indication that selling your home on eBay is still a long shot. We need real estate specialty sites, and there are only a few developed sites for true online real estate auctions. We will consider several sites and then, as a bonus, go to a final site where you can learn how to develop your own auction site.

Using the Major Auction Sites

For the premier real estate auction site on the Internet, in this author's opinion, go to this site:

www.realtynetbid.com

With over $1 billion in property auctioned, this site may be the future of real estate auctions on the Internet, especially at the higher end of the market.

Another potential winner in the online real estate auction arena is Homebid.com (*www.homebid.com*). Although this site is accepting property for auction only in Florida at the time of this writing (October 1999), look for this company to increase its auction presence online and in other markets.

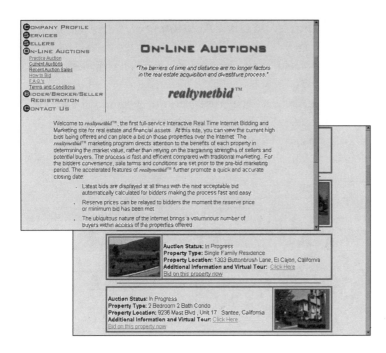

The realtynetbid online auction site provides a way for you to auction your investment property on the Internet.

There are many traditional auctioneers of real estate, and many have Web sites but do not conduct online auctions. Contacting one of these auction houses in your market area may be your best option for selling your property quickly, if you can get on their schedule quickly enough. A list of these traditional real estate auction houses can be easily and quickly found by going to this site and selecting the Real Estate category:

www.internetauctionlist.com

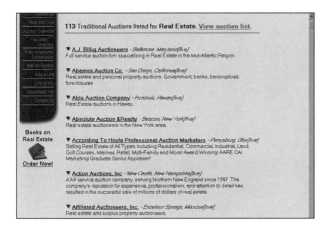

A traditional real estate auction house with an online presence may be your best source. A directory of these sites is found at www.internetauctionlist.com.

Conducting Your Own Auction

Real estate investors tend to be do-it-yourself types, and you just may want to hold your own online auction of your property. To find software and auction-hosting facilities, go back to the home page of the Internet Auction List at *www.internetauctionlist.com.* (See the following figure.) Look over their offerings for online auction software and auction hosting at this portal site for the online auction world. You just might end up developing your own real estate auction site.

This portal site to auctions on the Web offers auction software and hosting that could help real estate investors develop their own auction sites.

The Last Stop on Your Tour of e-Real Estate

You have made it to the end of our learning adventure, which has really been a breathless tour of e-real estate. From the overview through buying, selling, financing, and investing online, you have persevered in good cheer through many a long-winded speech from the tour guide. My hope is that you will have gained the knowledge and confidence to use the resources of the Internet in your next real estate transaction. Wishing you all the best in your endeavors, I look forward to receiving comments and suggestions online at *www.realestate-insider.com.*

PART V

Appendixes

APPENDIX A

Glossary of Real Estate and Mortgage Terms

A

abstract (of title)   A summary of the public records relating to the title for a particular piece of land. An attorney or title insurance company reviews an abstract of title to determine whether there are any title defects that must be cleared before a buyer can purchase the clear, marketable, and insurable title.

acceleration clause   A condition in a mortgage that may require the balance of the loan to become due immediately. The condition may be if regular mortgage payments are not made or for breach of some other condition of the mortgage.

agreement of sale   Known by various names such as *contract of purchase*, *purchase agreement*, or *sales agreement*, depending on location or jurisdiction. A contract in which a seller agrees to sell and a buyer agrees to buy, under specific terms and conditions spelled out in writing and signed by both parties.

amenity   A feature of the home or property that serves as a benefit to the buyer but that is not necessary to its use; may be natural (such as location, woods, or water) or man-made (such as a swimming pool or garden).

amortization   Repayment of a mortgage loan through equal monthly installments of principal and interest. The monthly payment amount is based on a schedule that allows you to own your home at the end of a specific time period (for example, 15 or 30 years).

Acknowledgement: The author gratefully acknowledges and sincerely thanks HUD and the American taxpayers for providing much of this glossary of terms. It has been ruthlessly edited, enhanced, and expanded by the author and Macmillan editors. Any errors or omissions, however, are certainly the fault of the U.S. government, its employees, and its contractors.

**Market Versus
Assessed Value:**
An appraiser deter-
mines the fair
market value of a
property; an assessor
determines the
assessed value.
The assessed value,
which may be lower
than market value, is
used for property
tax calculations.

annual percentage rate (APR)   Calculated by using a standard
formula, the APR shows the cost of a loan. Expressed as a yearly
interest rate, it includes the interest, points, mortgage insurance,
and other fees associated with the loan. Intended to provide a way
for consumers to compare actual financing costs of mortgages
between lenders.

application   The first step in the official loan-approval process.
This form is used to record important information about the
potential borrower necessary to the underwriting process.

appraisal   A document that gives an estimate of a property's fair
market value. An appraisal is generally required by a lender
before loan approval to ensure that the mortgage loan amount is
not more than the value of the property.

appraiser   A trained and licensed individual who uses his experience and knowledge to prepare the appraisal estimate.

ARM (adjustable rate mortgage)   A mortgage loan subject to
changes in interest rates. When rates change, ARM monthly payments increase or decrease at intervals determined by the lender.
The change in monthly payment amount, however, is usually subject to an interest rate cap.

assessor   A government official who is responsible for deter-
mining the value of a property for the purpose of taxation.

assumable mortgage   A mortgage that can be transferred from a
seller to a buyer. After the loan is assumed by the buyer, the seller
is no longer responsible for repaying it. There may be a fee or a
credit package involved in the transfer of an assumable mortgage.

assumption of mortgage   An obligation undertaken by the purchaser of a property to be personally liable for payment of an
existing mortgage. In an assumption, the purchaser is substituted
for the original mortgagor in the mortgage instrument, and the
original mortgagor is released from further liability in the
assumption; the mortgagee's consent is usually required.
The original mortgagor should obtain a written release from further liability if he desires to be fully released under the assumption. Failure to obtain such a release renders the original
mortgagor liable, if the person assuming the mortgage fails to
make the monthly payments.

An assumption of mortgage is often confused with *purchasing subject to a mortgage*. When someone purchases subject to a mortgage, the purchaser agrees to make the monthly mortgage payments on an existing mortgage, but the original mortgagor remains personally liable if the purchaser fails to make the monthly payments. Because the original mortgagor remains liable in case of default, the mortgagee's consent is not required to a sale subject to a mortgage. Both assumption of mortgage and purchasing subject to a mortgage are used to finance the sale of property. These methods may also be used when a mortgagor is in financial difficulty and desires to sell the property to avoid foreclosure.

B

balloon mortgage   A mortgage that typically offers low rates for an initial period of time (usually 5, 7, or 10) years. After that time period elapses, the balance is due or is refinanced by the borrower.

bankruptcy   A federal law whereby a person's assets are turned over to a trustee and used to pay off outstanding debts. This usually occurs when someone owes more than he has the ability to ever repay. Under the U.S. Bankruptcy Code, Chapter 7 covers full liquidation, Chapter 11 provides for reorganization of a bankrupt business, and Chapter 13 covers repayments of debts by individuals pursuant to a payment plan. A borrower desiring a mortgage normally must wait at least two years after being discharged from bankruptcy.

basis point   1/100 of 1 percent (.01%).

binder or **offer to purchase**   A preliminary agreement, secured by the payment of earnest money, between a buyer and a seller as an offer to purchase real estate. A binder secures the right to purchase real estate at agreed terms for a limited period of time. If the buyer changes his mind or is unable to purchase, the earnest money is forfeited—unless the binder expressly provides that it is to be refunded.

borrower   A person who has been approved to receive a loan and is then obligated to repay it and any additional fees according to the loan terms.

Fascinating Factoid:
The term *basis point* is used by bond traders, bankers, and other financial professionals to describe the fluctuations of bond yields, as in "the 30 year T-bond yield rose 20 basis points this month." You can use *basis point* at cocktail parties to impress members of the opposite sex with your financial acumen. Try "I made a bundle today on only a 5-basis-point move in T-bills."

bridal registry   A program supported by the FHA that allows a couple to open (register for) a bridal registry account into which family and friends can deposit gifts of cash. The funds in this account may then be used for a down payment on a house.

budget   A detailed record of all income earned and spent during a specific period of time. First-time homebuyers should develop a budget to account for the higher monthly cost of buying a home over renting.

building code   Based on agreed-upon safety standards within a specific area, a building code is a regulation that determines the design, construction, and materials used in building. New homes are inspected by local authorities to ensure that they meet code standards. A successfully inspected new home is issued a certificate of occupancy.

building line or **setback**   Distances from the ends or sides of the lot beyond which construction may not extend. The building line may be established by a filed plat of subdivision, by restrictive covenants in deeds or leases, by building codes, or by zoning ordinances.

C

cap   A limit, such as that placed on an adjustable rate mortgage, on how much a monthly payment or interest rate can increase or decrease.

cash reserves   A cash amount sometimes required to be held in reserve in addition to the down payment and closing costs. The amount is determined by the lender. FHA loans do not require cash reserves.

certificate of title   A certificate issued by a title company or a written opinion rendered by an attorney that the seller has good marketable and insurable title to the property that he is offering for sale. A certificate of title offers no protection against any hidden defects in the title that an examination of the records could not reveal. The issuer of a certificate of title is liable only for damages caused by negligence. The protection offered a homeowner under a certificate of title is not as great as that offered in a title insurance policy.

closing (or **closing day**)   Also known as *settlement*, this is the time at which the property is formally sold and transferred from the seller to the buyer. It is at this time that the borrower takes on the loan obligation, pays closing costs, and receives the title from the seller.

closing costs   The numerous expenses that buyers and sellers normally incur to complete a transaction in the transfer of ownership of real estate. These costs are in addition to the price of the property and are items prepaid at the closing between the buyer and the seller.

cloud (on title)   An outstanding claim or encumbrance that adversely affects the marketability of a title.

commission   Money paid to a real estate agent or broker by the seller as compensation for finding a buyer and completing the sale. Usually it is a percentage of the sale price—6 to 7 percent on houses, 10 percent on land.

condemnation   The taking of private property for public use by a government unit, against the will of the owner, but with payment of just compensation under the government's power of eminent domain. Condemnation may also be a determination by a governmental agency that a particular building is unsafe or unfit for use.

condominium   A form of ownership in which individuals purchase and own a unit of housing in a multiunit complex. The owners also share financial responsibility for common areas.

contract of purchase   *See* agreement of sale.

conventional loan   A private sector loan, one that is not guaranteed or insured by the U.S. government.

cooperative (co-op)   Residents purchase stock in a cooperative corporation that owns a structure. Each stockholder is then entitled to live in a specific unit of the structure and is responsible for paying a portion of the loan.

co-op sale   When two or more real estate agents split a commission on the sale of a listed property.

credit bureau score   A number representing the possibility that a borrower may default. The score is based on the credit history and is used to determine the borrower's ability to qualify for a mortgage loan. Scores range from 450 to 850; scores below 620 usually disqualify a borrower for a conventional loan.

credit history   The history of an individual's debt payment. Lenders use this information to gauge a potential borrower's ability to repay a loan.

credit report   A record that lists all past and present debts and the timeliness of their repayment. The report documents an individual's credit history.

D

debt-to-income ratio   A comparison of gross income to housing and non-housing expenses. With the FHA, the monthly mortgage payment should be no more than 29 percent of monthly gross income (before taxes); the mortgage payment combined with non-housing debts should not exceed 41 percent of income. Conventional loans normally have ratios of 28 percent and 36 percent for housing and total debt, respectively.

deed   A formal written instrument by which title to real property is transferred from one owner to another. The deed should contain an accurate description of the property being conveyed, should be signed and witnessed according to the laws of the state in which the property is located, and should be delivered to the purchaser on closing day. There are two parties to a deed: the *grantor* and the *grantee*. *See also* deed of trust, general warranty deed, quit-claim deed, and special warranty deed.

deed-in-lieu   To avoid foreclosure ("in lieu" of foreclosure), a deed is given to the lender to fulfill the obligation to repay the debt. This process doesn't allow the borrower to remain in the house, but it helps avoid the costs, time, and effort associated with foreclosure.

deed of trust   Like a mortgage, a security instrument whereby real property is given as security for a debt. However, in a deed of trust, there are three parties to the instrument: the *borrower*, the *trustee*, and the *lender* (or *beneficiary*). In such a transaction, the borrower transfers the legal title for the property to the trustee, who holds the property in trust as security for the payment of the debt to the lender or beneficiary. If the borrower pays the debt as agreed, the deed of trust becomes void. If the borrower defaults in the payment of the debt, however, the trustee may sell the property at a public sale, under the terms of the deed of trust. In most jurisdictions where the deed of trust is in force, the borrower is subject to having his property sold without benefit of legal proceedings. In recent years, a few states have begun to treat the deed of trust like a mortgage.

default   Failure to make mortgage payments as agreed in a commitment based on the terms and at the designated time set forth in the mortgage or deed of trust. It is the mortgagor's responsibility to remember the due date and send the payment before the due date, not after. Generally, if payment is not received 30 days after the due date, the mortgage is in default. In case of default, the mortgage may give the lender the right to accelerate payments, take possession, receive rents, and start foreclosure. Defaults may also come about by the failure to observe other conditions in the mortgage or deed of trust.

delinquency   Failure of a borrower to make timely mortgage payments under a loan agreement.

depreciation   Decline in value of a house caused by wear and tear, adverse changes in the neighborhood, or any other reason.

discount point   *See* point.

documentary stamps   A state tax, in the form of stamps, required on deeds and mortgages when a real estate title passes from one owner to another. The amount of stamps required varies with each state.

down payment   The portion of a home's purchase price that is paid in cash and is not part of the mortgage loan.

E

earnest money   The deposit money given to the seller or the seller's agent by the potential buyer upon the signing of the agreement of sale, to show that the buyer is serious about buying the house. If the sale goes through, the earnest money is applied against the down payment. If the sale does not go through,

Delinquent or Default?

Depending on the conditions stated in the promissory note and mortgage, a borrower can be in default *and* subject to foreclosure if payments are delinquent over 30 days.

the earnest money will be forfeited or lost unless the binder or offer to purchase expressly provides that it is refundable.

easement rights   A right-of-way granted to a person or company authorizing access to or over the owner's land. An electric company obtaining a right-of-way across private property is a common example.

EEM (Energy Efficient Mortgage)   An FHA program that helps homebuyers save money on utility bills by enabling them to finance the cost of adding energy-efficiency features to a new or existing home as part of the home purchase.

encroachment   An obstruction, building, or part of a building that intrudes beyond a legal boundary onto neighboring private or public land, or a building extending beyond the building line.

encumbrance   A legal right or interest in land that affects a good or clear title and that diminishes the land's value.
An encumbrance can take numerous forms, such as zoning ordinances, easement rights, claims, mortgages, liens, charges, a pending legal action, unpaid taxes, or restrictive convenants.
An encumbrance does not legally prevent transfer of the property to another. A title search is all that is usually done to reveal the existence of such encumbrances, and it is up to the buyer to determine whether he wants to purchase with the encumbrance or what can be done to remove it.

equity   The value of a homeowner's unencumbered interest in real estate. Equity is computed by subtracting from the property's fair market value the total of the unpaid mortgage balance and any outstanding liens or other debts against the property. A homeowner's equity increases as he pays off the mortgage or as the property appreciates in value. When the mortgage and all other debts against the property are paid in full, the homeowner has 100 percent equity in the property.

escrow   Funds paid by one party to another (the escrow agent) to hold until the occurrence of a specified event, after which the funds are released to a designated individual. In mortgage transactions, an escrow account usually refers to the funds a mortgagor pays the lender at the time of the periodic mortgage payments. The money is held in a trust fund, provided by the lender for the buyer. Such funds should be adequate to cover anticipated expenditures for mortgage insurance premiums, taxes, hazard insurance premiums, and special assessments.

escrow account   A separate account into which the lender puts a portion of each monthly mortgage payment. An escrow account provides the funds needed for such expenses as property taxes, homeowner's insurance, mortgage insurance, and so on.

F

Fair Housing Act   A law that prohibits discrimination in all facets of the homebuying process on the basis of race, color, national origin, religion, sex, familial status, or disability.

fair market value   The hypothetical price that a willing buyer and seller will agree on when they are acting freely, carefully, and with complete knowledge of the situation.

Fannie Mae   Federal National Mortgage Association (FNMA). A federally chartered enterprise owned by private stockholders that purchases residential mortgages and converts them into securities for sale to investors. By purchasing mortgages, Fannie Mae supplies funds that may be lent to potential homebuyers.

FHA (Federal Housing Administration)   A federal entity established in 1934 to advance homeownership opportunities for all Americans. The FHA assists homebuyers by providing mortgage insurance to lenders to cover most losses that may occur when a borrower defaults. This encourages lenders to make loans to borrowers who might not qualify for conventional mortgages.

FHLMC   *See* Freddie Mac.

first-lien position   The first recorded lien against a property is said to be in the *first-lien* position; the lien holder has a priority claim against the property over subsequently recorded liens. Normally, the first mortgage lender has first-lien position, and any second mortgage or home equity lender has second-lien position.

fixed-rate mortgage   A mortgage with payments that remain the same throughout the life of the loan because the interest rate and other terms are fixed and do not change.

flood insurance   Insurance that protects homeowners against losses from a flood. If a home is located in a flood plain, the lender will require flood insurance before approving a loan.

FNMA   *See* Fannie Mae.

foreclosure   A legal term applied to any of the various methods of enforcing payment of the debt secured by a mortgage or deed of trust, by taking and selling the mortgaged property and depriving the mortgagor of possession.

Freddie Mac   Federal Home Loan Mortgage Corporation (FHLMC). A federally chartered corporation that purchases residential mortgages, turns them into mortgage-backed securities, and sells them to investors. This provides lenders with funds for new homebuyers.

G

general warranty deed   A deed that not only conveys all the grantor's interests in and title to the property to the grantee, but also warrants that if the title is defective or has a "cloud" on it (such as mortgage claims, tax liens, title claims, judgments, or mechanic's liens against it), the grantee may hold the grantor liable.

Ginnie Mae   Government National Mortgage Association (GNMA). A government-owned corporation overseen by the U.S. Department of Housing and Urban Development. Ginnie Mae pools FHA-insured and VA-guaranteed loans to back securities for private investment. As with Fannie Mae and Freddie Mac, the investment income provides funding that may then be lent to eligible borrowers by lenders.

good faith estimate   An estimate of all closing fees, including prepaid and escrow items and lender charges. Such an estimate must be given to the borrower within three business days after submission of a loan application.

grantee   That party in the deed who is the buyer or recipient.

grantor   That party in the deed who is the seller or giver.

H

hazard insurance   Protects against damages caused to property by fire, windstorms, and other common hazards (the same as homeowner's insurance). The mortgagee is always the loss payee on the policy.

home inspection   An examination of the structure and mechanical systems to determine a home's safety. The inspection makes the potential homebuyer aware of any repairs that may be needed.

home warranty   Offers protection for mechanical systems and appliances against unexpected repairs not covered by homeowner's insurance. Coverage extends over a specific time period and does not cover the home's structure.

HUD   U.S. Department of Housing and Urban Development. The Office of Housing/Federal Housing Administration (FHA) within HUD insures home mortgage loans made by lenders and sets minimum standards for such homes.

HUD-1 Statement   Also known as the *settlement sheet*, this document itemizes all closing costs and accounts for the payment and receipts for all parties to the transaction. The document must be given to the borrower at or before closing.

HVAC   Heating, Ventilation, and Air Conditioning. A home's heating and cooling system.

I

index   A measurement used by lenders to determine changes to the interest rate charged on an adjustable rate mortgage. Common indices are the one-year U.S. Treasury T-bill rate and the LIBOR rate (London Inter Bank Offer Rate). Index rates can be found in *The Wall Street Journal*.

inflation   A decrease in purchasing power that occurs when the total amount of money and credit in an economy exceeds the total amount of goods and services available for purchase.

interest   A fee charged for the use of money.

interest rate   The amount of interest charged on loan, usually expressed as a percentage of the loan amount.

J

judgment   A legal decision. When requiring debt repayment, a judgment may include a property lien that secures the creditor's claim by providing a collateral source. Judgments must be paid before a mortgage loan can be funded, because a judgment can be (and often is) a prior lien. Mortgagees require a first-lien position.

L

lease purchase   Assists low-to-moderate–income homebuyers in purchasing a home by allowing them to lease a home with an option to buy. The rent payment is made up of the monthly rental payment plus an additional amount that is credited to an account for use as a down payment.

lien   A legal claim against property that must be satisfied when the property is sold. Specifically, a lien is a claim by one person on the property of another as security for money owed. Such claims may include obligations not met or satisfied, judgments, unpaid taxes, materials, or labor. *See also* special lien.

loan fraud   Purposely giving incorrect information on a loan application to better qualify for a loan. This act may result in civil liability or criminal penalties.

loan-to-value (LTV) ratio   A percentage calculated by dividing the amount borrowed by the price or appraised value of the home to be purchased. The higher the LTV, the less cash a borrower is required to pay as a down payment for the home.

lock-in   Because interest rates can change frequently, many lenders offer an interest rate lock-in that guarantees a specific interest rate if the loan is closed within a specific time. The lock-in period can range from 15 days to 120 days or longer, with the typical period being 30 days.

loss mitigation   A process to avoid foreclosure. The lender tries to help a borrower who has been unable to make loan payments and is in danger of defaulting on his or her loan.

loss payee   In a hazard insurance policy, this is the beneficiary. If a mortgage loan exists, the lender is always named as loss payee so that if the home (the collateral for the loan) is destroyed, the lender is paid by the insurance company.

M

margin   An amount the lender adds to an index to determine the interest rate on an adjustable rate mortgage. A typical margin might be 2.75 percent.

marketable title   A title that is free and clear of objectionable liens, clouds, or other title defects. A marketable title is one that enables the owner to sell his property freely to others and that others will accept without objection.

mortgage   A lien or claim against real property given by the buyer to the lender as security for money borrowed.

mortgage banker   A company that originates loans and resells them to secondary mortgage lenders such as Fannie Mae or Freddie Mac.

mortgage broker   An individual or firm that originates and processes loans for a number of lenders.

mortgage commitment   A written notice from the bank or other lending institution saying that it will advance mortgage funds in a specified amount to enable a buyer to purchase a house.

mortgage insurance   A policy that protects lenders against some or most of the losses that can occur when a borrower defaults on a mortgage loan. Mortgage insurance is required primarily for borrowers who have a down payment of less than 20 percent of the home's purchase price.

mortgage insurance premium (MIP)   A monthly payment—usually part of the mortgage payment—paid by a borrower for mortgage insurance.

mortgage modification   A loss-mitigation option that allows a borrower to refinance or extend the term of the mortgage loan and thus reduce the monthly payments.

mortgage note or **promissory note**   A written agreement to repay a loan. The agreement is secured by a mortgage, serves as proof of indebtedness, and states the manner in which the loan shall be paid. The note states the actual amount of the debt that the mortgage secures and renders the mortgagor personally responsible for repayment.

Dictionary Definition:

The term *mortgage* is a compound word formed by the Latin terms *mort* (dead) and *gage* (glove or hand, referring to a commitment, as in engagement). Its meaning is that you are entering a commitment that reaches beyond the grave. A chilling thought.

mortgagee   The lender in a mortgage agreement.

mortgagor   The borrower in a mortgage agreement.

O

offer   The indication by a potential buyer of a willingness to purchase a home at a specific price. The offer is generally put forth in writing. *See* purchase agreement.

origination   The process of preparing, submitting, and evaluating a loan application. This process generally includes a credit check, verification of employment, and a property appraisal.

origination fee   The charge for originating a loan. The fee is usually calculated in the form of points and is paid at closing.

P

partial claim   A loss-mitigation option offered by the FHA that allows a borrower, with help from a lender, to get an interest-free loan from HUD to bring his mortgage payments up-to-date.

PITI   Principal, Interest, Taxes and Insurance. The four elements of a monthly mortgage payment. Payments of principal and interest go directly toward repaying the loan; the portion that covers taxes and insurance (homeowner's and mortgage, if applicable) goes into an escrow account to cover the fees when they are due.

plat   A map or chart that shows the boundary lines, buildings, improvements on the land, and easements of a lot, subdivision, or community. Drawn by a surveyor.

PMI (Private Mortgage Insurance)   Privately owned companies offer affordable mortgage insurance programs for qualified borrowers. This insurance allows lenders to reduce their risk and offer up to 95 and 97 percent financing.

points   Sometimes called *discount points*. A point is one percent of the amount of the mortgage loan. For example, if a loan is for $100,000, one point is $1,000. Points are charged by a lender to raise the yield on the loan at a given note or coupon rate. Points paid may be used to reduce the note rate offered to a borrower. On a conventional mortgage, points may be paid by either the buyer or seller or may be split between them.

pre-approve   The lender commits to lend an amount to a potential borrower. The commitment remains in effect as long as the borrower meets the qualification requirements at the time of purchase.

pre-foreclosure sale   An event that allows a defaulting borrower to sell the mortgaged property to satisfy the loan and avoid foreclosure.

premium   An amount paid for insurance coverage on a regular schedule by a policyholder.

prepayment   Payment of a mortgage loan, or part of it, before the due date. Mortgage agreements often restrict the right of prepayment either by limiting the amount that can be prepaid in any one year or by charging a penalty for prepayment. The Federal Housing Administration does not permit such restrictions in FHA-insured mortgages.

prequalify   A lender informally determines the maximum amount an individual is eligible to borrow. This qualification is nonbinding and is not an approval or commitment to lend.

principal   The amount borrowed from a lender. The principal doesn't include interest or any other additional fees.

purchase agreement   *See* agreement of sale.

Q

quitclaim deed   A deed that transfers whatever interest the maker of the deed may have in a particular property. By accepting such a deed, the buyer assumes all the risks. Such a deed makes no warranties as to the title, but simply transfers to the buyer whatever interest the grantor has. Quitclaim deeds are often used to transfer a 50 percent undivided interest in a property from one spouse (who has 100 percent ownership) to another spouse. *See also* deed.

R

real estate agent   An individual who is licensed to negotiate and arrange real estate sales. The agent works for a real estate broker, who is normally licensed by the state to engage in real estate transactions.

Points and Buydowns:

Because points are paid in advance to a lender, they increase the yield or investment return on a note with a given note rate. Depending on market conditions, paying one point may allow the lender to reduce the note rate offered by about .125 to .250 percent. This is called *buying the rate down* or making a *permanent buydown.*

There is also a type of buydown known as a *temporary buydown.* In this case, a subsidy account is funded (usually by the seller or lender) to allow payments at a lower amortized rate for a specified period of time (one or two years). Typically, a temporary buydown is a 2/1—which means that the rate and calculated payments thereon are 2 percent lower than the permanent note rate for one year, then they are 1 percent lower for one year, then they are at the note rate for the remaining years of the loan. The subsidy account is used to make up for the below-market rate payments during the temporary buydown period.

Ask any loan officer to explain how buydowns are calculated. Better yet, for some fun, ask a real estate agent how a 2/1 buydown is calculated.

Know Your Restrictions:

The time to understand restrictive covenants is *before* you purchase a property with such covenants that run with the land. Don't assume that you'll be able to paint your house lime green, run your home-based business from the new property, or raise ferrets. Check the covenants before you buy.

REALTOR™   A real estate agent or broker who is a member of the National Association of Realtors and its local and state associations.

refinancing   Paying off one loan by obtaining another. Refinancing is generally done to secure better loan terms (such as a lower interest rate or shorter term).

rehabilitation mortgage   A mortgage that covers the costs of rehabilitating (repairing or improving) a property. Some rehabilitation mortgages, such as the FHA's 203(k) program, allow a borrower to combine the costs of rehabilitation and home purchase into one mortgage loan.

RESPA (Real Estate Settlement Procedures Act)   A law protecting consumers from abuses during the residential real estate purchase and loan processes by requiring lenders to disclose all settlement costs, practices, and relationships.

restrictive covenants   Private restrictions limiting the use of real property. Restrictive covenants are created by deed and may *run with the land*, binding all subsequent purchasers of the land, or may be *personal*, binding only between the original seller and buyer. The determination of whether a covenant runs with the land or is personal is governed by the language of the covenant, the intent of the parties, and the law in the state in which the land is situated. Restrictive covenants that run with the land are *encumbrances* and may affect the value and marketability of the title. Restrictive covenants may limit the density of buildings per acre; regulate the size, style, or price range of buildings to be erected; or prevent particular businesses from operating.

S

sales agreement   *See* agreement of sale.

settlement   Another term for *closing*.

special assessments   A special tax imposed on property, individual lots, or all property in the immediate area for road construction, sidewalks, sewers, street lights, and so on.

special forbearance   A loss-mitigation option in which the lender arranges a revised repayment plan for the borrower that may include a temporary reduction or suspension of monthly loan payments.

special lien   A lien that binds a specified piece of property (unlike a general lien, which is levied against all of one's assets). It creates a right to retain something of value belonging to another person as compensation for labor, material, or money expended on that person's behalf. In some localities, it is called a *particular lien* or a *specific lien*. *See also* lien.

special warranty deed   A deed in which the grantor conveys a title to the grantee and agrees to protect the grantee against title defects or claims asserted by the grantor and those persons whose right to assert a claim against the title arose during the period in which the grantor held the title to the property. In a special warranty deed, the grantor guarantees to the grantee that, during the time he has held title to the property, he has done nothing that has impaired the grantee's title or that might do so in the future.

subordinate   To place in a rank of lesser importance or to make one claim secondary to another.

survey   A map or plat made by a licensed surveyor showing the results of measuring a portion of land, with its elevations, improvements, and boundaries, as well as its relationship to surrounding tracts of land. A survey is often required by the lender to assure that a building is actually sited on the land according to its legal description.

sweat equity   Using labor to build or improve a property as part of the down payment. Sweat equity can be used for part of the down payment on purchases financed with FHA loans, but generally not with conventional loans.

T

title   As generally used, the rights of ownership and possession of particular property. In real estate usage, the title may refer to the instruments or documents by which a right of ownership is established (title documents), or it may refer to the ownership interest one has in the real estate.

Title I   An FHA-insured loan that allows a borrower to make non-luxury improvements (such as renovations or repairs) to the home. Title I loans of less than $7,500 don't require a property lien.

title insurance   A policy that protects lenders or homeowners against loss of their interest in the property caused by legal defects in the title. Title insurance may be issued to a mortgagee's title policy. Insurance benefits are paid only to the person named in the title policy, so it is important that an owner purchase an owner's title policy if he wants the protection of title insurance.

title search   A check of the title records, generally at the local courthouse, to make sure that the buyer is purchasing a house from the legal owner and that there are no liens, overdue special assessments, or other claims or outstanding restrictive convenants filed in the record that would adversely affect the marketability or value of the title.

trustee   A party who is given legal responsibility to hold the property in the best interest of or for the benefit of another. The trustee is placed in a position of responsibility for another, a responsibility enforceable in a court of law. *See* deed of trust.

Truth-in-Lending   A federal law obligating a lender to give full written disclosure of all fees, terms, and conditions associated with a loan, including an accurate calculation of the annual percentage rate (APR).

203(k)   An FHA mortgage insurance program that enables homebuyers to finance both the purchase of a house and the cost of its rehabilitation with a single mortgage loan.

U–Z

underwriting   The process of analyzing a loan application to determine the amount of risk involved in making the loan. The process includes a review of the potential borrower's credit history, the stability of his income, and a judgment of the property value.

VA (Department of Veterans Affairs)   A federal agency that guarantees loans made to veterans of the United States armed forces. Similar to mortgage insurance, a VA loan guarantee protects lenders against loss that may result if a borrower defaults.

zoning ordinances   The acts of an authorized local government that establish building codes and set forth regulations for property use.

APPENDIX B

Recommended Real Estate and Mortgage Web Sites

In this appendix, you will find loads of URLs, listed by the chapter to which the sites are relevant. Remember that the Web is constantly changing—and rapidly so. If any of these links fail to work, refer to this book's companion Web site, *www.realestate-insider.com*, where the same links can be found and will be kept current.

Chapter 1

Table B.1   A Brief Overview of Real Estate in a Networked World

URL	Description
www.bankrate.com/brm/rate/ mtg_home.asp	Mortgage rates from Bankrate.com
www.bankrate.com	Home page of Bank Rate Monitor
www.virtualrelocation.com/ index.html	Relocation information and link site
http://usacitylink.com/	Links to city-related sites
http://govinfo.kerr.orst. edu/usaco-stateis.html	Easy access to census data on U.S. counties
http://verticals.yahoo. com/cities/	Comparisons of cities on the basis of various criteria
http://venus.census.gov/ cdrom/lookup/	Access to detailed census data, down to zip code level
http://homefair.com/home/	Interesting relocation resource, but personal info is required to get some reports
http://govinfo.kerr. orst.edu/sddb-stateis.html	Quick access to school district data

continues

Table B.1   Continued

URL	Description
http://stats.bls.gov/cpihome.htm	Census lookup for Consumer Price Index (CPI) and other indices; difficult to use
http://www.census.gov/statab/www/	Online access to a statistical abstract of the U.S.; excellent for state, county, and MSA data and rankings by data element (such as crime or housing costs)
www.bloomberg.com	Top financial site; use it for tracking bond prices
www.hotbot.com	Author's favorite search engine

Chapter 2

Table B.2   For First-Time Homebuyers Only

URL	Description
www.mbaa.org/consumer	Consumer section of Mortgage Bankers Association of America; useful calculators and planning tools found here
www.financenter.com/homes_page.html	Best mortgage and financial planning tools on the Internet
www.eloan.com www.mortgage.com www.quicken.com www.loanworks.com	Online mortgage sites with good prequalifying capabilities
www.loanz.com	Online mortgage broker with good prequalifying features and free software
www.nehemiahprogram.org	Nehemiah Program home page; a non-profit organization that provides down payment gifts to FHA homebuyers
www.fairisaac.com	Source of credit scoring technology used by the mortgage industry; learn about credit scores here
www.creditinfocenter.com	Consumer credit advocacy site; info on credit scoring and credit repair
www.icreditreport.com	Get your credit report online here
www.ftc.gov/os/statutes/fcra.htm	Fair Credit Reporting Act found here; Sec. 611 is about correcting errors

URL	Description
www.equifax.com www.experian.com www.transunion.com	Home pages of the big three credit bureaus; interesting sites but no help for credit disputes
http://personalcredit.about.com	Try here for helpful info on credit repair

Chapter 3

Table B.3   For Buyers   How to Find Your Dream Home

URL	Description
www.realtor.com	Largest realtor listing site, with over 1.3 million listings
www.homeseekers.com	Second largest site with more than 680,000 listings
www.homeadvisor.com	MSN's listing site claims more than 500,000 listings
www.cyberhomes.com	Huge site with about 650,000 listings
www.homes.com	PCL Media's site has 300,000 listings from *Homes & Land* magazines
http://homescout.iown.com/scripts/ListingSearch.dll/Search	Direct link to iOwn multisite listing search engine (searches realtor *and* FSBO sites)
www.bamboo.com	Provides virtual tour technology to realtor listing sites; see examples here
www.ipix.com	Virtual tour technology enabler, available to all; see demo and check turnkey pricing here

Chapter 4

Table B.4   How to Find the Perfect FSBO Property

URL	Description
www.owners.com	Top FSBO listing site; the biggest and the best
www.buyowner.com	Another leading FSBO site
www.byowner.com	Another good FSBO site
www.by-owner-ol.com	A good FSBO site with many useful features, including email service
www.theschoolreport.com	School district info by county; free
www.fsboguide.com	Link site for finding FSBO listing sites in each state

continues

Table B.4: Continued

URL	Description
http://classifieds.yahoo.com/residential.html	Classified FSBO ads from Yahoo!
http://classifiedplus.aol.com	AOL's classifieds; find FSBO listing under Private Home Sales
www.realfind.com www.bonafideclassified.com	Newspaper Association of America's site provides access to online classifieds everywhere

Table B.5   Chapter 5   Sell Your Home Yourself and Save Thousands

URL	Description
http://realestate.yahoo.com/realestate/homevalues/ http://dowjones.homeprice check.com/top.html	Links to INPHO's home sale database for finding prior sales for comparable analysis
http://rhs.iown.com/buy/rh_buy_index.htm	iOwn.com's link to home price search with radius feature and mapping; extremely valuable free and $14.95 reports
www.propertyview.com	Comparable sale price report with up to 30 properties for $9.95
www.fsbotips.com	Good source of FSBO marketing information and downloadable reports
www.homegain.com	Source of seller information, with free library of articles
www.owners.com	Best FSBO site for sellers; free and paid listings with pictures
www.freehomelistings.com	Free FSBO site; no picture; list until sold
www.homeportfoliojunction.com (Advanced Real Estate Listing Service)	Free FSBO site; 1 picture; list until sold; many upgrades; paid packages and services, including Web page
www.fsboworldnet.com	Free FSBO site; 1 picture; list until sold; donation of $10 or more to homeless organization requested
www.comprealty.com	Free FSBO site; no picture; 6-month listing; upgrade 1 photo $39; upgrade 2-5 photos $59

URL	Description
www.advertise-free.com	Free FSBO site; no picture, 90-day listing; upgrade to 1 photo $5; upgrade to 2 photos $8; upgrade to 3 photos $10
www.dotcomusa.com	Free FSBO site; no picture; 30-day listing; free email notice when listing is viewed
www.forsalebyownernetwork.com	Free FSBO site; 1 picture; list until sold
www.homesaledirect.com	FSBO site; 30 days free, 1 photo scanned for you or 6 uploaded; upgrade $19.95 for list until sold
www.theadnet.com	Free classified ad–style listing; no picture; deleted after 30 days
www.efsbo.com	60-day free classified listing; no picture; upgrades available
www.by-owner-ol.com	Paid FSBO site; 3 package deals (see text)
www.buyowner.com	Paid FSBO site; $79 for 8 pictures; list until sold.
www.fsbo.com	FSBO site with good package deal
www.vrrealty.com	San Francisco Real Estate site featuring virtual tour technology
www.spree.com www.homestead.com www.tripod.com www.webjump.com http://geocities.yahoo.com/home www.angelfire.com www.hotbot.com	Free Web-hosting and page-creation services are available at these sites
www.emailaddresses.com	Directory of hundreds of free email sites
www.hotbot.com www.hotmail.com www.mail.com www.yahoo.com	Some free email sites
www.messageclick.com	Free fax and voicemail using email

Chapter 6

Table B.6   Helping Your Realtor Sell Your Home

URL	Description
www.homegain.com	Useful selling tools plus anonymous agent evaluation service

continues

Table B.6: Continued

URL	Description
www.arello.org	Find real estate licensing authorities in each state, except Minnesota, Wisconsin, and Rhode Island
www.iown.com/selling/index.html	Use the AgentFinder link here to find agents with a radius search around a city or within a zip code

Chapter 7

Table B.7   Financing Your Dream Home

URL	Description
www.bloomberg.com/markets/rates.html	Direct link to mortgage rates on Bloomberg's service
www.mortgage101.com	Mortgage rates by state
www.mortgagequotes.com	Good place for comparison rate shopping
www.interest.com	Compare and shop rates with an unsorted list
http://mortgage.quicken.com	Quicken's mortgage referral site; 15+ lenders per state
http://homeadvisor.msn.com	Microsoft Network's mortgage referral site
www.iown.com	Leading online broker site; shop rates with two clicks
www.eloan.com	E-LOAN, leading online mortgage banker/broker
www.keystroke.com	Online broker with access to over 200 lenders; affiliate of Pacific Guarantee Mortgage
www.mortgage.com	Grandaddy of online mortgage bankers, funding $2 billion per year
www.interloan.com	Full service conventional online mortgage banker (no FHA or VA)
www.fanniemae.com/singlefamily/products/markets/emerging_markets.html www.homepath.com	Direct link to Fannie Mae's products for first-time homebuyers; HomePath has a list of lenders for these products in your state
www.freddiemac.com/sell/expmkts/98online.html	Direct link to Freddie Mac's first-time homebuyer product line

URL	Description
www.homesteps.com	Freddie Mac's site for sales of fore-closed properties with special financing for first-time homebuyers
www.fhatoday.com	Online FHA lender site where you can learn about and apply for an FHA loan
www.vba.va.gov/bln/loan/ LGYINFO.HTM	If you are a veteran, go straight into VA's loan information area with this link
www.hud.gov/buyhome.html	HUD's extensive information for first-time homebuyers
www.hud.gov/mortprog.html	Direct link to information about fed-erally insured mortgage programs, including FHA mortgages
www.nehemiahprogram.com	Go here for information on the Nehemiah down payment gift pro-gram and to find a participating lender
www.lendingtree.com	Four offers for loans within 48 hours after you apply
www.loanweb.com	Lenders will bid for your loan
www.mortgageauction.com	Service of RealEstate.com; 250 lenders bid for your business
www.clnet.com	Lenders respond to your loan listing on Computer Loan Network's site

Chapter 8

Table B.8   Applying for Your Mortgage Online

URL	Description
www.eloan.com	E-LOAN's online application is easy but must be done in one session.
www.mortgage.com	Mortgage.com lets you save and quit and return later during the applica-tion.
www.iown.com	iOwn.com's 7-part application is sim-ple to complete with stop, restart, and review features.

Chapter 9

Table B.9   How to Find Bargain Properties Online

URL	Description
www.realfind.com	Online classified ads from your local newspaper are a good place to search for bargain properties.
www.brucebates.com	Home of the Bates Foreclosure Report (monthly subscription); limited free searches.
www.bankhomes.net	ForeclosureNet subscription site for foreclosure listings; limited free searches.
www.4close.com	Foreclosures Online subscription site; limited free searches.
www.all-foreclosure.com	Foreclosure info site with links to other listing sites.
www.johntreed.com/realestate.html	Real estate author and expert John T. Reed debunks the real estate gurus you see on infomercials.
www.homesteps.com	Freddie Mac's Real Estate Owned (REO) site.
www.fanniemae.com/homes/index.html	Fannie Mae's REO site.
www.premierereo.com/pas_properties.html	Premiere Asset Services REO site.
www.bankofamerica.com	Bank of America's REO site.
www.bankreo.com/bankreo/reoframe.htm	Search for REO properties foreclosed by OCWEN.
www.hud.gov/local/sams/ctznhome.html	Find HUD foreclosures here.
www.vba.va.gov/bln/loan/homes.htm	Start here to search for VA foreclosures.
http://propertydisposal.gsa.gov/property/	Find surplus government real estate at auction here.
www.treas.gov/auctions/customs	Buy a drug dealer's house at auction from the Feds.

Chapter 10

Table B.10   Financing Investment Property

URL	Description
www.loansurfer.com	Investor loans to 80% LTV on single-family only

URL	Description
www.iown.com www.eloan.com	Both iOwn and E-LOAN offer 90% LTV investor loans on 1- to 4-family residential property
www.lendingtree.com	Let lenders bid on your investor loan requirements
www.mortgagerates.com/features/index.html	Search for investor-friendly lenders in your state
www.creonline.com	Find real estate investor clubs in your state here
www.galaresources.com	Hard money lender with minimum loan amount of $50,000
www.guardianmortgage.com	New York commercial lender for your big deals; minimum loan $750,000
www.blackburne.com	Search for a source to fund your deal in a directory of 750 commercial lenders

Chapter 11

Table B.11   Use the Net to Market Investment Property

URL	Description
www.quickmortgage.com	Investor-friendly nationwide lender with 100% LTV programs
www.nehemiahprogram.com	Source for down payment gifts for FHA buyers
www.noteworthyusa.com	Portal to the world of note buying and selling
www.papersourceonline.com	Cash flow industry's leading newsletter publisher
http://notenetwork.com	American's Note Network lets you list your note for sale
www.bostonnote.com	Major direct note buyer
www.chasefinancial.org www.nationalcontractbuyers.com www.realestatenotes.com	More note buyers
www.notefinders.com	Note listing site
www.realtynetbid.com	Premier online real estate auction site
www.homebid.com	Growing real estate auction site
www.internetauctionlist.com	Portal site to the universe of online auctions and auction technology on the Web

APPENDIX C

The RealEstate-Insider.com Companion Site

Your decision to purchase this book demonstrates your interest in both real estate and the Internet. Although the real estate industry does evolve and change, its pace is glacial compared to the dramatic rate of change and growth of the Internet, e-commerce, and the supporting technologies. The multimedia capabilities of the World Wide Web, from panoramic graphics to streaming video and audio, are perfect for marketing real estate. Virtual tours are just beginning to appear on listing sites. Online real estate is the "killer app" of the Internet for the near term.

To keep you current on e-real estate (and to keep this book fresh and up-to-date), the author maintains a companion Web site for the book and a portal for access to real estate resources on the Internet. Visit the site at *www.realestate-insider.com*.

Here you will find links to every site documented in this book. The links are maintained to ensure the book's links work for you in the future. Because the site provides accurate, current hyperlinks organized by chapter, you can read the book and then go to the chapter heading on the site to easily follow the examples.

In addition to support for the book, readers can subscribe to the author's free email newsletter, *Insider's Guide to Online Real Estate*, download free software, and find links to other useful real estate resources. Topical areas on the site eventually will include the following and more:

- Internet real estate news

- FSBO listing sites

- Realtor listing sites

- Mortgage resources

- Real estate investing resources

- First-time homebuyer information

- Credit and credit repair online

- Relocation guide

- Buyers' forum

- Sellers' forum

- Investors' forum

- Real estate and mortgage software directory

- The Real Estate Insider Store

One of the goals of the site is to become the leading consumer-oriented real estate portal on the Net. Readers of *Sams Teach Yourself e-Real Estate Today* can make a valuable contribution to consumer awareness by reporting positive and negative experiences with online real estate and mortgage sites and companies. Postings from consumers about their online real estate experiences, about new sites and services, and about successes and failures will be archived for everyone's benefit.

You're Safe:

Because the site has a consumer focus, and because it advocates and encourages for-sale-by-owner activity, individual real estate agent and brokerage advertising and site links will be carefully segregated and identified. The email newsletter subscriber list will never be rented or disclosed to any real estate agent or broker. The only way a real estate agent will get your email address is if you provide it. Your private information will never be released to real estate agents, brokers, or mortgage companies, period.

Site nomination by readers and newsletter subscribers will help this portal site grow in scope and value to consumers. Your participation is encouraged. The author appreciates and looks forward to your support and involvement. See you online!

INDEX

It's
Here!

The IT site
you asked for...

InformIT is a complete online library
delivering information, technology,
reference, training, news and opinion to IT
professionals, students and corporate users.

Find IT Solutions Here!

www.informit.com

Tell Us What You Think!

As the reader of this book, you are our most important critic and commentator. We value your opinion and want to know what we're doing right, what we could do better, what areas you'd like to see us publish in, and any other words of wisdom you're willing to pass our way.

You can fax, email, or write me directly to let me know what you did or didn't like about this book—as well as what we can do to make our books stronger.

Please note that I cannot help you with technical problems related to the topic of this book, and that due to the high volume of mail I receive, I might not be able to reply to every message.

When you write, please be sure to include this book's title and author as well as your name and phone or fax number. I will carefully review your comments and share them with the author and editors who worked on the book.

Fax: 317-581-4770

Email: *internet_sams@mcp.com*

Mail: Mark Taber
         Associate Publisher
         Sams Publishing
         201 West 103rd Street
         Indianapolis, IN 46290 USA

Yourself
Today

Sams Teach Yourself
e-Travel Today

Planning Vacations, Finding Bargains, and Booking Reservations Online

Mark Orwoll
ISBN: 0-672-31822-9
$17.99 US/$26.95 CAN

Other Sams Teach Yourself Today Titles

e-Trading
Tiernan Ray
ISBN: 0-672-31821-0
$17.99 US/$26.95 CAN

e-Personal Finance
Ken and Daria Dolan
ISBN: 0-672-31879-2
$17.99 US/$26.95 CAN

e-Music
Brandon Barber
ISBN: 0-672-31855-5
$17.99 US/$26.95 CAN

e-Banking
Mary Dixon and Brian Nixon
ISBN: 0-672-31882-2
$17.99 US/$26.95 CAN

e-Job Hunting
Eric Schlesinger and Susan Musich
ISBN: 0-672-31817-2
$17.99 US/$26.95 CAN

e-Parenting
Evelyn and Karin Petersen
ISBN: 0-672-31818-0
$17.99 US/$26.95 CAN

All prices are subject to change.

SAMS

www.samspublishing.com